To my friend & p...
Elspeth Bissett,
on the occasion
of our first success.

—— A GUIDE TO ——
VANITY FAIR

C.C.
31 · iii · 1995

—A GUIDE TO—
VANITY FAIR

Charles Cleall

ABERDEEN UNIVERSITY PRESS

First published 1982
Aberdeen University Press
A member of the Pergamon Group
© Charles Cleall 1982

British Library Cataloguing in Publication Data

Cleall, Charles
  A guide to Vanity Fair.
  1. Thackeray, William M. Vanity Fair
  I. Title
  823'.8   PR5618

ISBN 0-08-028474-4

Printed in Great Britain
The University Press
Aberdeen

CONTENTS

FOREWORD

In 1976, I got out of my car to look at a secondhand-book stall, and purchased for 5p a copy in perfect condition of what I have come to regard as the most lively story I ever read. Its vocabulary is enormous; so that, by page 249, I began making notes in the margin, and perusing works of reference to gather material to help me understand the text. Having begun it, there came a point when I felt it sensible to type out what I had learned, and to expand it so that the story could be enjoyed by readers of an age which has so much in common with the cut and thrust of that of Thackeray's characters, for all its unlikeness.

It will be noted that most of the words defined have a pocket etymology; a habit into which pupils of Mr W D James at Hampton School were apt to get, and for which they came to pay him tribute as adding greatly to their enjoyment of language. In general, the oldest root is given, and the meaning of that root where traceable. Words occurring several times are defined several times - and (perhaps disconcertingly at first) not always in the same way; partly because that would be dull; partly because they were actually looked up afresh each time, and sometimes in different sources: so that the reader becomes aware that words are explained differently by different philologists, and that definitions are in some measure a matter of conjecture (not a bad thing to find out). I trust that this feature will prove enjoyable rather than irritating: it should certainly prove instructive.

Thanks and acknowledgements are due for help in tracing recondite historical figures to James A Pratt, ALA; for help in ascertaining the meaning of words other than English to James B Caird, Herbert W Smith and Gordon H Turner; and for reading many literary works aloud with me over the years to my wife, Mary, and my daughters, Mrs David M Lindsay and Mrs Grant J Nicol.

CHARLES CLEALL
Milltimber

THE STORY OF ´VANITY FAIR´

In a letter to his mother, Thackeray tells us what sort of story he set out to write.

> What I want is to make a set of people living without God in the world (only that is a cant phrase); greedy, pompous men; perfectly satisfied, for the most part, and at ease about their superior virtue. Dobbin and poor Briggs are the only people with real humility as yet. Amelia´s is to come, when her scoundrel of a husband is well dead with a ball in his odious bowels; when she has had sufferings, a child, and a religion: but she has at present a quality above most people; viz, LOVE; by which she shall be saved.

His attitude has continually a shaft of humour. In the letter quoted, he actually wrote, not ´viz´ [abbreviation for the Latin word, Videlicet, ´namely´] but ´whizz´ - intending the same meaning, but simply having fun while he conveyed it. In his book, Thackeray: Prodigal Genius, John Carey suggests that, in this first novel, Thackeray was mercilessly and sardonically himself, making wicked fun. Later, for fear of affecting his income or social position, he was more careful what he wrote, and kept everything within polite bounds; but Vanity Fair gives us an almost intoxicatingly sharp picture of what it felt like to be alive in the first half of the nineteenth century.

Without thinking much about it, he uses an enormous vocabulary; much bigger than almost any writer who expects to be widely read today; and phrases from Latin, Greek, French, German and Italian.

Some editors have taken out every word and phrase not easily grasped by young readers, and substituted works and phrases which are; but the result is soft and spiritless to the point of insipidity. Vanity Fair is delightfully wicked! and the wickedness has to be left in if we are to have an appetite for so long a story; so the words and phrases must stay - but they need a glossary to help us to grasp them; and that is what this little work attempts to provide.

The story is not without surprises; so much so that, at times, we wonder whether we can believe what we are reading. Hence, for those who would like it, here is the story in brief.

SYNOPSIS

Amelia Sedley, who comes from a comfortable home, has reached the last day of her education at Miss Pinkerton's Academy for Young Ladies. Presented with a copy of Dr. Johnson's dictionary she goes home for good; but, to tide her over the first few weeks of her new state, she takes her friend and fellow-pupil, Rebecca Sharp, whose background is not so comfortable - and not nearly so respectable.

Once in Amelia's home, Rebecca flirts with Amelia's elder brother, Joseph (known as Jos), who has a well-paid post in the East India Company; which was founded by a group of merchants in London who received a charter from Queen Elizabeth I in 1600, and permission from the Mogul Emperor in 1611 to establish trading posts in India (its powers were considerable, and taken over by the Crown in 1858). Amelia (a little surprisingly for a girl still at school - for she was, till today) is engaged to be married to Lieutenant George Osborne (her lifelong friend); and he and his old school-friend, Captain William Dobbin, are amused at Rebecca's hopes of a rich marriage, but George talks to Jos so spitefully about Rebecca that he leaves London to avoid her.

Rebecca (whom we may call Becky, for everyone else does) takes up appointment as governess to the eight- and ten-year-old daughters of Sir Pitt and Lady Crawley, of Queen's Crawley in Hampshire; not at all the sort of couple we might expect, for Sir Pitt is an old, dirty and selfish man, and Lady Crawley (his second wife, and humbly born) is afraid of him.

Sir Pitt's younger son, Captain Rawdon Crawley, is attracted to Becky; and his rich aunt, Miss Crawley, decides to raise her socially at least to the level of a companion. When Miss Crawley falls ill, Becky travels with her to London, and nurses her back to health - and secretly marries Rawdon. Lady Crawley dies, and Sir Pitt proposes to Becky, who has to confess that she is married to Rawdon. Miss Crawley, outraged that Becky should find any other patron, refuses to have anything to do with her, and cuts Rawdon out of her will. When she dies, her money goes to Rawdon's mean and straitlaced elder brother, Pitt, who eventually succeeds to the baronetcy.

Amelia's father, John Sedley, loses his money; and George's father (despite having christened his son George Sedley Osborne) forbids George to marry Amelia, and indicates his wish that George should marry Amelia's former fellow-pupil, a rich coloured girl from the Leeward Islands, named Miss Swartz. At her father's behest, Amelia prepares to release George from his engagement; but Captain Dobbin (who has secretly worshipped Amelia ever since he met her) persuades George to marry Amelia in secret, and visits old Mr Osborne to explain why the marriage was bound in honour to have taken place. Mr Osborne is not bound in honour, and decides that George shall cease effectually to be his son (though he arranges for George to receive a further £2000). George goes with Captain Dobbin and Rawdon to the battle of Waterloo, and is killed in it.

Amelia bears a son, whom she names after his father, and lives with her parents close to poverty. Small sums of money (which she assumes come from her brother, but which come in fact from Captain Dobbin) keep them from debt. Rawdon and Becky live by their wits, and Becky is determined to conquer fashionable London, aided by the powerful but sinister Marquis of Steyne. Rawdon dotes on his little son, in whom Becky has no interest. Discovering his wife's intrigue with Lord Steyne, Rawdon takes back her money and her jewels, leaves little Rawdon with his brother and sister-in-law, Sir Pitt the younger and Lady Crawley, and goes abroad as governor of the illfated Coventry Island.

Shunned by society, Becky makes a new life (of sorts) on the Continent. Old Mr Sedley's affairs decline so sadly that Amelia, for her son's sake, gives little Georgy into the guardianship of old Mr Osborne, who refuses to have anything to do with her. Mrs. Sedley dies, and Jos, returning from India, sets up his father and sister in happier circumstances, where Captain Dobbin nerves himself to propose to Amelia, and is refused.

Mr Osborne dies, leaving Amelia an annuity, and little Georgy rich. The two of them go with Jos and Captain Dobbin to Pumpernickel in Thuringia. Here, they meet Becky, who regains her ascendancy over Amelia; at which Captain Dobbin protests. Amelia spurns him, and he returns to England.

Becky decides that it is time for her to do a good deed for a change, and proves to Amelia that her husband had tried to persuade Becky to run away with him just before he was killed. Amelia realizes where her affections truly lie, and eventually marries Captain Dobbin. Rawdon is made a baronet, but dies soon afterwards, and little Rawdon becomes the second baronet; but neither he nor anyone except Jos will associate with Becky. Having given Becky control of his money, Jos dies - in suspicious circumstances.

In case the reader is using an edition which omits the information, it must be said that <u>Vanity Fair: A Novel without a Hero</u> was written by William Makepeace Thackeray (1811-1863), and first published in twenty monthly instalments from January 1847 to July 1848. The action of the story takes place during the years 1814-1830, in London, Queen's Crawley (an invented village in Hampshire), Brighton, Brussels, Paris, India, Pumpernickel (Thackeray's name for Weimar, now in East Germany: 51°N 11°E) and Ostend. The reader may find that the story gains by reference to an atlas of these countries, and to an illustration of the points of the compass, and by looking through the notes before reading the chapter (unless it be long).

BEFORE THE CURTAIN

Thackeray does not plunge us straight into the story, but talks himself into it, so to speak. He is himself the Manager, of course.

BUCKS   = Dandies.

QUACKS   = Short for quacksalvers - ignorant pretenders to medical knowledge
            [German Quakeln, 'to chatter or prattle' + Salbe, 'healing ointment'];
            so the quacks peddled ointment, and had a line of patter to persuade
            passers-by that they needed it.

TUMBLERS = Gymnasts; acrobats.

MUMBLING HIS BONE = Chewing or biting softly with toothless gums.

ESCHEW   = Avoid [Old English Sceoh, 'afraid'].

This introduction is curiously like the opening credits of a television film; even to picturing the leading characters, but in a distant way, as though whetting our appetite before bringing them to life.

CHAPTER 1

SEMIRAMIS = An Assyrian queen of the ninth century before Christ, noted for her wisdom and beauty (and for having built the city of Nineveh).

MRS CHAPONE = Hester Chapone (born Hester Mulso), 1727-1801, was noted for her 'Letters on Improvement of the Mind' (1772). She used to write for The Rambler and Gentleman's Magazine.

BOW-POT = a version of 'bough-pot' - a vase containing small boughs, ferns or flowers.

GILLYFLOWER=WATER = water scented by steeping (soaking) of wall-flowers or clove-scented pinks.

BILLET = document or letter [from the Anglo-Latin Billetta; the diminutive of Billa, from Latin Bull, 'seal': 'a little seal': hence, a sealed document].

ORTHOGRAPHY = spelling [Latin for 'correct writing'].

DIXONARY = spelt thus to show how Miss Pinkerton believed that refined people would pronounce the work 'dictionary'.

MINERVA = the Roman goddess of wisdom, whom the Greeks called Pallas Athene.

MRS [JAMES] BILLINGTON = an opera singer who lived from 1782 to 1811. Born Elizabeth Weichsel, she had a range of three octaves, with 'exquisitely beautiful high notes' but 'limited powers of expression'.

HILLISBERG OR PARISOT = French dancers at the Haymarket Theatre.

MULATTO = the child of a negro and a European ['young mule'; a mule being the off-spring of a horse and an ass].

TIPSIFY = to make drunk, and so cause to tip (or fall over).

SAL VOLATILE = 'volatile salt'; that is, smelling salts (of ammonium carbonate).

FILAGREE = 'wrought' [from Filigrane: Latin Filum, 'thread' + Granum, 'grain'; meaning originally delicate work with threads and beads, and eventually any delicate or finely woven work].

1

HAPLY = by chance; 'as it happened'.

SENSIBILITY = sensitiveness.

ROUND-HAND = copy-book writing, or cursive.

TWADDLING = trifling; empty; not amounting to anything.

EBULLITIONS = outbursts [Latin _Ebullire_, to boil over].

BANDBOX = Cardboard (or thin-wood) box for collars and hats (originally for the bands or ruffs of the seventeenth century).

MADEMOISELLE, JE VIENS VOUS FAIRE MES ADIEUX = 'Ma'am, I come to bid you goodbye'.

TURBAN = an Oriental head-dress [Persian _Dulband_] worn by women in Britain in the eighteenth and early nineteenth centuries.

CHISWICK MALL = a sheltered walk [from _Mall_; the alley in which a game called Mall (which uses balls and mallets) was played].

CHAPTER 2

DR RAINE = Matthew Raine, headmaster of the public school called Charterhouse from 1791 to 1811.

BEAK OF A WHERRY = the prow (or tip) of a light rowing-boat.

PLACABLE = gentle; easy to please (originally ´pleasing´; as grateful meant ´giving cause for gratitude´, and hopeful meant ´giving cause for hope´).

MISANTHROPIST = hater of mankind [Greek Misein, ´to hate´ + Anthropos, ´man´].

PROPENSITY = tendency [Latin Propensus, ´inclined´].

ENTRECHATS = A pun on the ballet manoeuvre in which the heels are struck together during an upward leap.

DELIRIUM TREMENS = a fever caused most often by drinking alcohol.

BAILIFFS = Debt-collectors; sheriff´s deputies. [Latin Bājulāre, to carry´].

PRECOCITY = grown up ahead of one´s years [Latin Pre-, ´before time´ + Coquere, ´to ripen´]

DUN = Person employed to collect debts (that is, unlike the bailiff, not an officer of the court) [the word was taken from the town of Dunkirk, and meant at first a ship from that town, and then a privateer - that is, a ship privately owned, but armed, and authorized by the government to be used in war].

INGENUE = An inexperienced girl, with the implication that she is frank, open, and easily impressed.

MR LAWRENCE OR PRESIDENT WEST = Thomas Lawrence (1769-1830), President of the Royal Academy in 1820; Benjamin West (1738-1820) was his predecessor from 1792.

CONVENTUAL = Like that of a convent (which is governed by the ringing of bells at regular intervals.

REPROBATE = Rejected as worthless [Latin Re-, ´Deny´ + Probāre, ´To test; ´to approve´].

3

CREOLE = West Indian of European or negro descent [Spanish <u>Criollo</u>, 'One born in the locality'].

ROUTED = Put to flight [Latin <u>Rupta</u>, 'Broken],

INDENTURES = Contract between a school and a pupil-teacher; any contract [originally in duplicate on one skin, cut jaggedly in two].

AFFIDAVIT = A sworn statement [Latin for 'he has sworn'].

TURNPIKE = Toll-gate [originally a defensive frame set with pikes, or metal spikes].

DRAWING-ROOM = The room where debutantes where presented at Court: short for 'withdrawing-room'.

GIMCRACKS = Trivial possessions.

CORNELIAN = Precious stone of reddish white or deep, dull red, after the colour of the cornelian cherry; a type of chalcedony (or quartz) used for seals (as for sealing-wax).

SPRIGGED MUSLIN = Fine cotton fabric (said to have come originally from Mosul: a town in Iraq, some 115 miles north by west of Baghdad) decorated with woven sprigs or sprays.

CASHMERE SHAWLS = from Kashmir in Northern India.

NABOBS = Civil officers [from Urdu <u>Nawwāb</u>, 'Deputy governor'].

CHAPTER 3

BUCKSKINS = Deerskin breeches.

HESSIAN BOOTS = High boots with tassels in front at the top (first worn by the troops of Hesse in east-west Germany).

CROWN PIECES = Silver coins rather larger than a fifty-pence piece.

BUGGY = Two-wheeled, horse-drawn vehicle.

PALANQUIN = Covered litter (or portable bed - as in the French Lit) carried by four men.

PILLAU = Boiled rice and meat, with butter, spices and raisins [Persian Pilaw, pronouced 'peelaff'].

TURBOT = A large flat-fish [Old English Thornbut, 'prickly flatfish'].

BEAU = Man who pays excessive attention to his clothing, manner and manners.

TOXOPHILITE = Archery [from Roger Ascham's book, Toxophilus - 'lover of the bow' - published in 1545, to promote physical education].

GUTHRIE'S GEOGRAPHY = William Guthrie's New Geographical, Historical and Commercial Grammar was in use for more than a century.

'BLUEBEARD' = An opera (1798) by George Colman & Michael Kelly.

ALNASCHAR = A beggar (in The Arabian Nights) who dreamed that he married the daughter of the Vizier (or chief minister of state [from Arabic Wazir, 'State councillor]).

ORIENTAL CLUB = An actual club founded in 1824 at 18 Hanover Square W1.

COCKED HAT = A three-cornered hat with the brim turned permanently up [that is, cocked, or 'set erect'].

BRUMMEL = George Bryan Brummel, 1778 - 1840.

BUCKS = Men devoted to setting or following the fashion in clothes, manner and manners.

METROPOLIS = Greek for ´mother city´; here, London.

BLUE-PILL = Pill for biliousness, or upset stomach.

BON-VIVANT = One fond of good living (that is, living comfortably; richly; luxuriously).

AMOUR-PROPRE = Self-respect.

INDOLENCE = Self-indulgence [Latin for ´no pains].

POMATUMS = Ointments (in the sense of hair-cream), in which Pomata (or apples) were said once to have been an ingredient.

FINIKIN = Fussy; over-exacting [previously Finical; probably from Fine in the sense of ´subtle; intricate; delicate´].

TOILETTES = Preparations to go out [from the ´little nets´ which have been covers for dressing-tables for many, many years, and eventually gave their name to the purposes of dressing-tables - and other ceremonies].

COQUETTE = Woman who likes men to find her attractive.

CHILI = the pod of a capsicum, or pepper.

MORTIFICATION = Feelings of humiliation [´Being made to die´].

CAPITAL = Excellent.

CAYENNE = A very pungent powder obtained from dried and ground pods of capsicum [native name, from Tupi in Brazil].

SETTING HER CAP AT YOU = Trying to marry you

ROUT-CAKES = Dainties for an evening party or reception.

CHAPTER 4

VAUXHALL = Originally, Falkes's Hall (after Falkes de Breauté, lord of the manor in the thirteenth century); famous for its 'new' Spring Gardens, 1650-1859, which replaced the old gardens at the north-east corner of St. James's Park.

PARRICIDE = A father-killer [Latin Parricīda; from Pater + Cīda].

EXETER 'CHANGE (or EXCHANGE) = A circus with a celebrated elephant (the building was demolished in 1829).

CHINTZ = Originally chints; cotton cloths printed with designs in at least five different colours - usually flower-designs - and subsequently glazed [Persian Chinz, 'stained']: such cloths, if really good, are now printed in twenty-three colours.

DOUBLÉ = Over-hung ['doubled'].

CALICO = White or unprinted cotton cloth [from the town of Calicut, on the west coast of India, some 385 miles south of Bombay, whence the cloth was first introduced: 11°N, 76°E].

CURTAIN LECTURE = 'Reproof given by a wife to her husband in bed' (from Dr Johnson's dictionary).

TÊTE-A-TÊTE = In intimate conversation [literally, 'head-to-head'].

HOBBADYHOY = Now 'hobbledehoy': a youth between boyhood and manhood, at 'the awkward stage'.

GIG = A light, two-wheeled, one-horse carriage.

CHAUSSURE = Footwear

MEDULLA = William Howell's Medulla ['compendium' or 'summary'] Historiae Anglicanae ['of English history'], 1679.

OTTOMANS = Cushioned seats like sofas, but without backs or arms [from Othoman; the Sultan who laid the foundation of the Turkish empire in Asia].

PUNKAHS = Large fans made from palmyra leaves, or of cloths stretched on frames suspended from the ceiling [Hindi <u>Pankha</u>, ´fan´].

TATTIES = Screens, usually made of the roots of the fragrant cuscus grass, filling a window or door-way, and kept moist to freshen the room [Hindi <u>Tatti</u>]

MAHOUT = Elephant-driver [Hindi <u>Mahaut</u>].

<u>**AIDES-DE-CAMP**</u> = Officers assisting a general on the battle-field.

<u>**SEHNSUCHT NACH DER LIEBE**</u> = Longing for love [German].

TARS = Sailors (who at this time wore their hair in pig-tails, which they daubed with tar to keep them done up).

<u>**LAGRIME**</u> = Tears [Italian].

<u>**SOSPIRI**</u> = Sighs [Italian].

<u>**FELICITA**</u> = Ecstasy [Italian].

LATTICE = Short for ´lattice-window´, made of strips at right angles to each other, holding small panes of glass [French <u>Lattis</u>, lath].

HAPLESS = Luckless; unfortunate [Icelandic <u>Happ</u>, ´good fortune´].

<u>**CUTCHERRY**</u> = Here, office hours [from Hindi <u>Kachahri</u>, ´hall of audience´; hence, business office].

<u>**DISTINGUEE**</u> = Distinguished [French].

FILAGREE = Here, silver [See Chapter 1].

<u>**BILLET-DOUX**</u> = Love-letter [French].

TIFFIN = Here (as in India), lunch [from eighteenth-century slang <u>Tiffing</u>, ´eating or drinking other than at meal times´ - meal times being breakfast and dinner (evening meal)].

CHAPTER 5

BRUITED = Noised [from <u>Bruire</u>, ´to roar´: French];   reported; rumoured.

HARDBAKE = Almond toffee.

POLONIES = Sausages made of partly cooked pork (originally from the Italian town of Bologna, which gave them their name).

PRIMER = Schoolbook.

REPEATER = Chiming watch.

MR KEAN TO MR KEMBLE = John Philip Kemble (1757-1823) and Edmund Kean (1787-1833).

<u>ARABIAN NIGHTS</u> = A collection of stories written in Arabic, entitled ´The Thousand and One Nights´, which became known when Antoine Galland translated them into French in 1704-1708. They were not translated into English till 1840 (by Edward William Lane); so that Dobbin must have read them in French.

<u>AS IN PRAESENTI</u> = Latin grammar (from a heading in the textbook used at Eton College).

PEACHED = Told (tales); informed ¿aphetic form - that is, without the unaccented vowel at its beginning - of Appeach, ´to accuse´; from the French <u>Empechier</u> (Latin <u>Impedicare</u>, ´to catch; entangle; put into fetters´)].

RUMSHRUB = Drink made from rum, sugar and lime, lemon or orange juice [Arabic <u>Shurb</u>, ´drink´; from <u>Sharaba</u>, ´to drink´: cf Sherbert, syrup, &c].

KNOUT = A type of whip [Russian <u>Knut</u>, ´scourge´].

RENCONTRE = Conflict [French <u>Rencontrer</u>, ´to meet´].

NAPIER = Sir William Napier (1785-1860) wrote a history of the Peninsular War.

BELL´S LIFE = A London sporting newspaper (as we see from chapter 54).

COCK = Champion boxer.

USHER = Assistant master (originally, ´door-man´ - Latin <u>Ostiārius</u>´).

TELÉMAQUE = The Greek hero Telemachus, whose story was told by Francois de Salignac de la Mothe Fenelon (1651-1715). This presentation heightens our impression that Dobbin liked reading stories in French. Note that Dobbin´s Christian name is given in its Latin version for the presentation; a practice in grammar schools.

ORSON/VALENTINE = Twin brothers in a folk tale, who were said to have been abandoned in the woods in their infancy. Valentine was found, and brought up at Court; but Orson grew up in the den of a bear. In young manhood, they met and fought, and became friends after Valentine had subdued Orson.

LITTLE WARBLERS = A song-book for children.

<u>VAINQUEUR</u> = Conquering; attempting to vanquish or impress [French].

A GAWKY = A gawk; a simpleton or booby; a stupid, awkward fellow [Scottish <u>Gowk</u>, ´cuckoo´; also ´clumsy person; clown´].

<u>NAIVETÉ</u> = Artlessness; simplicity; ´green-ness´; inexperience [French: pronounced ´nigh-eve-te].

<u>AH, MON BEAU MONSIEUR</u> = ´Ah! my fine fellow´.

GAUGE = Measure (´I have you weighed up´).

FROGGED COAT = Coat fastened by tassels or large buttons passed through loops [Portuguese <u>Froco</u>, ´tag´].

GAZETTED = Announced in <u>The London Gazette</u> (where all such appointments are still printed) as appointed to command a company of soldiers.

BUMPER = Glass filled to the brim.

PRIMING = filling with liquor.

CHAPTER 6

FEMME DE CHAMBRE = Lady's maid (a distinctly superior servant).

BRAGGADOCIO = Empty, idle, boastful [pronounced '-doh-chee-oh'].

BODKIN = Wedged in where there is really only room for two.

SATE = The old spelling of what we now spell 'sat'.

BUCK = Dashing fellow; dandy.

GREYS = Grey horses.

BURTHEN = The original poetic form of 'burden' [Old English Byrthen, 'that which is carried'].

COCKNEYS = Contemptuous term (meaning 'cock's egg') for a native of London (traditionally, 'one born within the sound of the bells of the church of St Clement, Bow'): probably from the expression 'cock's egg' being applied to small, mis-shapen eggs, and eventually to small, mis-shapen people (as Londoners tended to be).

MADAME SAQUI = A tight-rope dancer (1786-1866) acclaimed by Napoleon as 'premiere acrobate de France'. She did not in fact appear at Vauxhall till 1816.

STOUT = Strong, dark brown bitter beer brewed from malt partly charred by being dried at high temperature (malt is grain which has been steeped in water to cause it to sprout).

DE TROP = In the way [French].

RACK PUNCH = The aphetic form of 'arrack punch'; meaning spirits mixed with hot water, lemons, sugar and spice - the spirits having been distilled from rice and the fermented sap of the coconut and other palm trees [Arabic Araqa, 'to sweat'].

GOURMAND = Glutton [French].

MAUDLIN = Weepy; sentimental (alluding to paintings of St Mary Magdalene - Magdalene being pronounced 'maudlin' till recent years).

DANIEL LAMBERT = The fattest man in English history (1770-1809), who died at St Margaret's, Leicester, weighing 52 stone, 11 pounds. He was a lightweight compared with Robert Earl Hughes, who died at Bremen, Iowa, U S A, in 1958, weighing 76 stone, 5 pounds.

TOP-BOOTS = High boots having a top of light-coloured leather.

SODA-WATER = In fact, invented in the eighteenth century, and praised by Cavallo in an essay published in 1798.

SMALL BEER = A weak type of beer.

BACCHANALIAN = A person in the habit of drunken revelry [Bacchus was the Roman god of wine].

ASKANCE = Sideways (in other words, they exchanged glances, as people do when they do not entirely approve of what they hear or see).

MOLYNEUX = A French boxer mentioned in Boxiana by Pierce Egan (1772-1849) in 1812. He is mentioned again in Chapter 34.

MESALLIANCE = An unsuitable marriage [French].

DISCOMFITED = Frustrated; disappointed; defeated [Latin Dis-, 'Not' + Conficere, 'to achieve'].

MIEN = Manner or appearance; bearing [Arminian Min, 'face'].

APOTHECARY = What we should now call a pharmacist; in the centuries before this, the seller of medicines prescribed them [Late Latin Apothecarius, 'shop-keeper'].

BANTERED = Made fun of.

ORPHAN OF THE FOREST = J I M Stewart suggests that Thackeray is thinking of William Diamond's novel, The Foundling of the Forest.

RETICULES = Handbags; work-bags.

FICHUS = Head-scarves.

TAGS = Pieces of metal at the ends of laces.

BOBBINS = Pieces of wood round which yard or thread was wound.

FALLALS = Pieces of finery.

SPENSER = Close-fitting bodice or jacket modified from the over-coat without tails given vogue by the second Earl Spencer, 1758-1834.

CHAPTER 7

ROTTEN (BOROUGH) = A town with special privileges conferred by royal charter, and a municipal corporation: a town which sends members to Parliament: so-called if it had decayed to a handful of voters, but still retained its electoral privileges - and M P.

IMPEACHED FOR = Charged with; accused of [Latin In-, 'into' + Pes 'foot'; unbelievable as it must sound, 'to trap someone by getting him to put his foot in it' (Late Latin Impedicāre)].

PECULATION = Misappropriation of public funds [Latin Pecūlāri, 'to embezzle']; spending public money as if it were one's own.

DUNDAS = Henry Dundas (1742-1811) became the first Viscount Melville, after service in William Pitt's government.

MR WROUGHTON = An actor said not to have appeared at Covent Garden after 1785 (before Rebecca could have seen him).

APOLOGUE = Fable; story [Greek]. The fable, of course, is one by Aesop (a Greek of the sixth century before Christ).

HATCHMENT = A tablet bearing the coat of arms of someone who has died (altered from 'achievement', which, in heraldry, means a coat of arms, or 'escutcheon', commemorating some notable feat, with chapeau, coronet, helm, crest, mantling, motto, supporters and compartment [see Simple Heraldry]).

INTERSTICES OF = Spaces between [Latin Inter-, 'between' + Stitium, 'standing'].

PERQUISITES = Something obtained from an appointment in addition to its wages or salary [Latin Perquisītum, 'Sought diligently'].

TURKEY CARPET = Carpet woven in one piece of richly coloured wools, imported from Turkey (or in imitation of a Turkish carpet).

BROWN HOLLAND = Unbleached linen fabric (originally from Holland).

CELLARET = Sideboard with compartments for bottles of wine.

DUMB WAITER = Upright pole with revolving trays for dishes and cruets, now sometimes called a 'lazy Susan'.

CRABBED = Uninviting.

ATTENUATED = Worn-out [Latin for 'beaten out thin'].

PORTER = Dark beer made from charred malt, named after the workmen among whom it was a favourite.

FARDEN = Farthing; quarter of an old penny (the present penny being worth 2.4 old pence) [Anglo-Saxon Feorthing, 'a quarter'; from Feortha, ' a fourth'].

BOARD WAGES = Wages which kept servants in food and drink while the family was away, and there were few duties or appearances to keep up.

RUSHLIGHT = A candle of feeble power, made by dipping the pith of a rush (or reed) in grease.

SAMPLER = Originally 'Exemplar' - a piece of embroidery worth copying (or the copy made of it by a beginner).

DEFUNCT = Dead [Latin Defunctus est, 'He has completely done with (life)'].

ROSEATE = Rose-coloured; pink.

'NECKS = J I M Stewart says, a coaching inn called 'The Swan with Three Necks'.

BENJAMINS = Overcoats named after the tailor who designed them.

'CHANGE = Exchange demolished in 1829 (mentioned in Chapter IV); a building where merchants, brokers and bankers did business.

OLD WELLER = Tony Weller, father of Sam Weller (in Dickens's Pickwick Papers, 1836).

JACK SHEPPARD = A highwayman (1702-1724) hanged at Tyburn - now Marble Arch.

BUCEPHALUS = The horse of Alexander the Great (356-323 BC; King of Macedon from 336 BC till his death).

DIVAGATION = Wandering about [Latin Dīvāgor, 'to wander about'].

CHAPTER 8

HIND = Farm bailiff, who looks after the estate. [Middle English <u>Hine</u>; from <u>Hina</u> ´members of a household´].

DISTRAINING= Forcing someone to meet his obligations, or pay his debts, by seizing and retaining something he owns [Latin <u>Dis-</u>, ´apart´ + <u>Stringere</u>, ´To draw tightly´].

HUSSEY = Originally ´housewife´; an impolite form of address indicating contempt.

UDOLPHO = From Mrs William Radcliffe´s novel, <u>The Mysteries of Udolpho</u> (1794).

STAYS = A kind of waistcoat with pieces of whalebone to give the body support (Rebecca is hinting that the ancestors were fat).

CHITS = Young people [Anglo-Saxon <u>Cith</u>, ´shoot or twig´].

ODIOUS = Hateful [Latin <u>Odiōsus</u>].

HORSE-LAUGH = A loud, coarse laugh.

CASE-BOTTLE = A bottle (often square in shape) made to go in a carrying-case with other bottles.

CRIBBAGE = A game for two, three or four people, using the whole of a pack of playing-cards. It gets its name from the crib, or pair or cards given to the dealer by each player.

HARANGUING = Loud speaking [literally, to a ring of people, from the Old High German <u>Hring</u>, ´a circle´].

EXPOUNDING = Explaining [Latin <u>Expōnere</u>, ´to set forth´].

TIPSY = Muddled with strong drink.

WORSTED = A type of wool first made at Worstead in Norfolk.

MOUNTS = Puts on.

CAP AND BELLS = The ornaments of a clown.

SHOVEL-HAT = Stiff, broad-brimmed hat, with the brim turned up at the sides, worn by important clergymen.

GREDIN = Rascal [French].

MONSTRE = Monster [French].

INFAMES = Infamous; notorious; shameful [French].

ANGLAIS = English [French].

COSSACKS = Warlike horsemen from the southern steppes of Russia [Turkish Kazak, ´robber´].

VENT = Outlet [Old French Fente, ´cleft´].

SILENUS = A satyr in Greek myths who was always drunk.

CHAPTER 9

PAS = Precedence; pride of place [French].

DRAGGLED = Made dirty being dragged along the ground.

SLATTERNLY = Untidy [slang Slatter, 'to spill carelessly'].

LANGUID = Drooping [Latin Languēre, 'to be faint'].

EGRESS = Exit, going out [Latin Ē-, 'out' + Gradior, 'to step'].

FLUX = Flow [Latin].

CARTE-BLANCHE = Full discretionary power [French].

ALIENI APPETENS, SUI PROFUSUS = 'Covetous of other people's [property], lavish with his own' (Sallust)].

PARSIMONY = Careful expenditure [Latin Parsimōnia, 'frugality'].

DEBRETT = The who's who of noble families.

BOOR = Country bumpkin; ill-mannered person [Anglo-Saxon (Ge)bur, 'countryman'].

PETTIFOGGING = Going to law for trivial or vexatious reasons.

LOZENGE = Panel bearing a coat of arms.

CHAPTER 10

INDOLENT = The opposite of ´painstaking´ [Latin ´Not suffering´].

CRÉBILLON = Claude Prosper Crébillon (1707-77) wrote popular but improper stories.

SMOLLETT = Tobias George Smollett (1721-71) was a Scottish novelist who wrote a history of England.

SEQUESTERED = Secluded; set apart [Latin Sequestrāre, ´to put in safe keeping´].

CAMILLA = A Volscian princess (the Volscians were an ancient, warlike tribe who lived in Latium; the part of Italy where Rome is; whom the Romans conquered in the fourth century before Christ) who was so fleet of foot that she could run over a field of corn without bending the blades, and over the sea without wetting her feet, according to Virgil (70-19 BC), the greatest of the Latin poets.

WITHAL = Likewise; moreover; in addition; in spite of that.

PECCADILLOES = Trifling offences [Spanish].

CONSTRUE = Translate [Latin Construere, ´to assemble; put together´].

PROFANE = Here, other than sacred [Latin Pro-, in the sense ´outside´ + Fānum, ´the temple´].

ÉMIGRÉES = People who have left their home-land [French].

D´HOZIER´S DICTIONARY = Louis Pierre D´Hozier´s General Armorial of France, published in six volumes, 1738-68; later expanded to ten volumes, and subtitled, A Register of French Nobility.

BACK-GAMMON = A game for two, played with pieces or ´men´, and dice, on a table or board made for the purpose [Danish Bakke, ´tray´ + Gammen, ´mirth´].

COUNT DE TRIC-TRAC = Joke: tric-trac is a form of back-gammon.

ABBÉ DU CORNET = Another joke: cornet a des means ´dice-box´.

DRAGOON = Soldier from a cavalry regiment [French <u>Dragon</u>, ´carbine´; so named because it breathed fire - a carbine is like a musket, but shorter].

PRETERMIT = To let pass without notice; to leave undone [Latin <u>Praetermittere</u>, ´to let pass´].

<u>BEL ESPRIT</u> = A pretty wit (someone who said things not only humorous but neat).

ST JUST = Probably Louis Antoine Léon St Just (1767-1794), a French revolutionary.

MR FOX = Charles James Fox (1749-1806) was a strenuous opponent of the war with France.

FLUNG A MAIN = In the dice-game of hazard, a number from 5 to 9 was called by the dicer before casting the dice: this was the ´main´.

PULING = Pining; weak [French <u>Piauler</u>, ´to whine´].

CHAPTER 11

BRUISERS = Prize-fighters.

COURSING MATCH = Probably, of greyhounds hunting a hare.

VISITATION DINNER = Dinner in honour of the official visitor (for example, the Sovereign is the Visitor of Westminster Abbey).

GIG-LAMPS = The lanterns of his two-wheeled carriage.

PEPPER-AND-SALT FROCK = A long coat or tunic woven of white with black or brown dots.

REVERSIONARY SPOIL = Money or land granted to someone, which reverts to the granter when the other dies.

GLOBES = Spheres covered with a map. There were terrestrial globes for geography, and celestial globes for astronomy.

SPUD = Three-pronged fork.

TOADY = Servile dependant: So-called because accomplices of quack-doctors would pretend to swallow toads (thought to be poisonous) and the quacks purport to cure them.

MR & MRS GLAUBER = Rebecca is being sarcastic. Johannes Rudolph Glauber (1603-88) was a famous German physician whose salts (sulphate of soda) were taken like Epsom salts.

PELISSES = Garments worn out of doors by young children over their other clothes.

PUT = Blockhead; duffer; stupid man [Welsh Pwt, ´short, thick person´].

CHAW-BACON = Country bumpkin (who chews bacon).

APOPLEXY = A stroke (usually brought about by a clot of blood stopping the circulation) [Greek Apoplēxia, ´To strike and disable´].

BLACKAMOOR = Originally 'black moor', or negro, in the sense of a native of Mauritania in NW Africa (20°N, 10°W).

DES FRAICHES TOILETTES = New accessories [French].

REVERSION OF THE LIVING = Here, the right to become the next Rector of Crawley.

CROSS [THE FIGHT] = Fix; arrange beforehand who was going to win [slang].

TROUVAILLE = Godsend [French].

PARAGON = Someone who is excellent in every way [French].

PICK THIS DRESS OF MINE = Unpick it; take it to pieces.

PHILANTHROPIST (sarcastic; meaning the opposite) = One who loves the human race [Greek Phile-ein, 'To love' + Anthropos, 'Man'].

MILLINERY = [Look after her] hats, gloves and ribbons [originally, a milliner was a Milaner - someone who came from Milan in Italy. Later, a milliner was one who sold the hats, gloves and ribbons such as Milaners sold].

CRIBLE DE DETTES = Heavily in debt [French].

WATTIER'S AND THE COCOA-TREE = Wattier's was solely a gaming club (what we should now call a casino), 1806 - 1819. The Cocoa Tree (64 St. James's St) was a gaming club at this time, but had been a coffee-house from 1698, and a Tory stronghold in turn before being re-established as a club in 1853.

MESS = The hall (usually large and grandly furnished) in which officers took their meals [from Old French Mes, 'article of food'; hence, in the army or navy, a party taking meals together, and eventually where those meals were taken].

DEPÔT = The headquarters of a regiment [Latin Depositum, 'a thing laid down or stored'].

WICKET = Gate [French Guichet, 'wicket-gate'].

SHIP = Sheep (to show how Sir Pitt pronounced the word).

CHAPTER 12

FADE = Ordinary; commonplace; uninteresting [French].

INSIPID = Dull; uninteresting [Latin In -, 'Not' + Sapidus, 'Tasty'].

MANGNALL'S QUESTIONS = Miss Richmal Mangnall (1769-1820) was headmistress of a girls' school at Wakefield in Yorkshire. Her Questions, used in many girls' schools, reached their eighty-fourth edition (and an edition signifies not simply a reprinting, but a bringing-up-to-date by altering whatever has been found to be incorrect) in 1857, and were reprinted as recently as 1892.

RATTLING = Playing loudly (slang).

HERZ-MANNER = Henri Herz (1806-88) of Vienna taught piano at Paris Conservatoire from 1842-1874; so the 'Herz-manner' was the manner in which he would play sonatas (Paris Conservatoire is notorious for the hard touch of her pianists).

PETIT MINOIS CHIFFONNÉ = Pleasant but irregular little features (literally, 'crumpled').

INVIOLABLE = Here, secret; not to be written about or revealed.

THE FOUNDLING = The Foundling Hospital; or, to give it its full name, 'The Hospital for the maintenance & education of exposed and deserted young children' (a hospital being originally 'a place giving hospitality'); was the work of Thomas Coram (1688-1751). The building beginning in 1739, the foundation stone was laid in the chapel on 1 May 1747. Handel, asked to participate in the opening ceremony on 1 May 1750, offered to give an organ for the chapel, and to conduct a performance of Messiah (the most famous oratorio, or long piece of sacred music, ever written). So many attended the ceremony that a repeat performance was given on 15 May, and annually thereafter till Handel's death (with the composer conducting); from 1760 to 1768, conducted by J C Smith; and from 1769 to 1777 conducted by John Stanley. A photograph of the chapel is on the page facing page 448 in the Oxford Companion to Music (tenth edition).

The site of the Hospital was in Guilford Street, London WC1 [see Geographers' London Atlas, page 59, 4E]; actually on what the atlas shows as Coram's Fields playground. In 1926, the building was taken down, and rebuilt at Redhill, and moved in 1935 a second time to Berkhamstead (on the Chesham Road). All that remains of the original is a number of memorials; some at Guilford Street, and some at the offices of the Thomas Coram Foundation, 40 Brunswick Square WC1 (adjoining Guilford Street). Charles Dickens rented a pew in the original chapel. The present hospital at Berkhamstead is known as Ashlyn's School.

COTILLON = A brisk dance [French].

CARLTON HOUSE = London residence of His Royal Highness the Prince Regent (who became George IV, and ruled the country while his father was mentally ill).

MUSLIN = A fine cotton fabric [from Mosul 38°N, 43°E in Iraq, 125 miles north north-west of Baghdad, where the fabric was formerly made].

SPENCER = Strictly, a short, close-fitting jacket trimmed with fur: perhaps, here, such trimmings. Originally, a man's outer coat without skirts, as worn by the second Earl Spencer, 1758-1834.

CHAPTER 13

BAND-NOTE = Misprint for bank-note? Perhaps connected with the Bond (or promise to pay) printed on all such notes.

LIAISON = Here, an embarrassingly close link or connection [Latin Ligāre, ´to bind´].

ENSIGN = Formerly the flag- or standard-bearer; now the rank of second lieutenant.

ADMIRABLE CRICHTON = James Crichton (1560-85?) was called admirabilis (´marvellous´) in Johnston´s Heroes Scoti (´Great men of Scotland´), 1603.

HARRIDAN = An impolite term for an elderly woman [French Haridelle, ´old horse´).

BIVOUACKING = Camping overnight without tents [French].

AMBROSIAL = Heavenly [Greek A-, ´not´ + (M)brotos, ´mortal´].

BREVET = Nominal only, without extra pay [French for ´Warrant´; meaning the document conferring such rank on an officer]. Sambo, like many who approve of an officer, is speaking of him as though he has a higher rank than he possesses.

SWAIN = A young rustic; a lover [Old Icelandic Sveinn, ´lad´].

SUBSCRIBER = To the monthly issues of Vanity Fair, which was first published in instalments.

MILKSOP = Effeminate young man.

OLD SLAUGHTERS´ = A famous coffee-house.

IPHIGENIA = The daughter of the Greek hero Agamemnon (in Homer´s story of the Trojan horse), who died at Aulis (a small hill above the bay in which the Greek fleet was becalmed); according to Aeschylus, at her father´s hands. In other accounts, she was snatched away by the goddess Artemis, who substituted a hind (a bear/a calf) for Agamemnon to sacrifice instead.

BILLINGSGATE = The world´s most famous fish-market, in London.

<u>REPERTOIRE</u> = Set of pieces practised till they are ready to play to an audience [French].

PIPE = A measure of wine containing 126 gallons (virtually 73 litres).

COMMANDER-IN-CHIEF = His Royal Highness The Duke of York, younger son of King George III.

FILBERTS = Hazel nuts; which generally ripen by St Phil**bert's** Day (22 August).

COLLOQUY = talk together [Latin].

CHAPTER 14

LOZENGE ON THE PANELS = A figure, diamond-shaped, containing a coat of arms, on the doors [French Losange, from the Spanish Losa, ´a slate or paving-stone´].

CRIMPLED = Artifical, by means of a hot-iron called a crimping-iron (said to be a lighter form of Cramped, meaning ´contracted´ or ´shrunk´ - as when a swimmer gets cramp, and his legs pain him because the calf-muscles are staying contracted in a spasm.

RUMBLE = What became known as the dickey-seat: the hind part of a carriage, when arranged to seat passengers (not popular, because it was meant for servants: its name imitated the noise of the carriage, which was heard more clearly there than by other passengers).

EQUIPAGE = Carriage and horses [French].

PHYSICIAN AND MEDICAL MAN = Two people, of whom the physician was superior. The inferior was the apothecary, who made up medicines as well as prescribing them (like the pharmacists of today, in making them up; but a pharmacist does not prescribe them - does not decide which medicines the patient needs).

ANTIPHLOGISTIC = To counter inflammation [Greek].

CHARGER = War horse.

DAME DE COMPAGNIE = [Paid] companion [French].

FEMME DE CHAMBRE = Not, as might be thought, the chamber-maid, but a lady´s maid - a distinctly superior serving-woman [French].

BLACKGUARD BOYS = Originally, lowly servants who hauled the coal in wealthy households. Here, probably grubby little boys are meant.

CURVETED = Pranced; in partiicular, raising both forelegs, and, as they fall, both hind-legs [Latin Curvāre, ´to bend´].

CONDIMENT = Seasoning [Latin Condimentum].

SALTS-BOTTLE = Smelling-salts.

PLACABLE = Capable of being soothed, pacified or pleased with little effort on anyone else's part.

GRUEL-BASIN = Bowl of oatmeal broth, or thin porridge [Old French Gruel, from the older word Grutel, from Dutch Grut. The strange thing is that there is an English word which came directly from the Dutch: Grout (compare with the American word Grits): all meaning pounded barley, wheat or maize, to make porridge].

'OFF THE HOOKS' = Short for 'dropped off the hooks'; meaning dead [slang. A word is slang when it does not actually mean what it says, or anything like it, but something decided on to mystify people outside the circle which uses it].

APPROPINQUITY = Nearness [Latin Appropinquare, 'to draw near; to approach'].

RALLIED = Teased [French Railler, 'to banter'].

DROLL = Comical; ludicrous; laughable [Gaelic, 'a slow, awkward person'].

WAGGISH = Humorous; witty [Short for Waghalter: 'one likely to end on the gallows'; that is, to 'wag', or swing to and fro, from a 'halter': a hempen rope].

SNEAK = Twister; underhand fellow. (Anglo-Saxon Snican, 'to creep')

WHYOU = 'Whew!' (low whistle of disgust).

EXPOSTULATIONS = Urgent pleas [Latin Exposcere, 'To demand of anyone'].

ROUTED = Put to flight; broken up in disorder [French Route, 'a portion broken off'].

FRANK = A signature which, being that of a Member of Parliament, caused the envelope it was written on to be delivered free of charge [French Franc, 'free', like the Franks of old, who were never enslaved].

AMANUENSIS = Writer; here, one who writes down the message of another [Latin, 'clerk'; 'secretary'].

A SINECURE = It was paid for, but required no work [Latin, 'without care'].

DEMISE = Death [French Demettre, 'to put aside; to lay off'].

FLAT = Fool; silly fellow.

DEUCE = Devil [perhaps from Latin Deus, 'god', used as an exclamation].

INAMORATO = Strictly, a male lover. Captain Crawley, had he been less ignorant, had said inamorata [Italian, from Latin In-, 'in' + Amor, 'love'], meaning 'beloved' or 'sweetheart'.

PIQUET = Card-game for two, using 32 cards (the low cards, values 2 to 6, being excluded).

REPAST EN GARCON = Bachelor dinner [French].

TIN = Money [slang].

SWAGGER = Insolent, defiant way of walking [from Swag, 'to move as though swinging to and fro'].

PERSIFFLED = Teased him unmercifully [French Persifler, 'to banter'. The word Persiflage means 'frivolous or jeering talk'].

ENTRE-NOUS = Between ourselves [French].

HATCHMENT = Altered from Achievement, meaning an escutcheon; a square or diamond-shaped tablet bearing a coat of arms (often, of a person who has died).

ENGOUMENT = Infatuation; state of foolish adoration [French].

CRAPE = Plainly woven, highly twisted raw silk, with a crisped surface; in black, worn as mourning [French Crepe, 'crisp'].

CHAPTER 15

PIGAULT LE BRUN = Charles Pigault le Brun (1753-1835), who wrote novels about love.

THE PRINCE REGENT'S DIVORCE = The Prince Regent became King George IV in 1820, and was never divorced (though Parliament nearly debated a Bill to let him have one).

TENDRE = Tenderness; affection; liking; love [French].

DOTER = Give a dowry [wedding gift] to [French].

PROPENSITIES = Inclinations [Latin].

ÉCLAIRCISSEMENT = Enlightenment; understanding [French]; we should probably say, 'When it dawns on her ...'

DIE = In late popular Latin, 'something given by Fortune' [Dātum]; here, one of a pair of dice [which are thrown in pairs].

MA TANTE = My aunt [French].

PORTEUS'S SERMONS = Sermons by The Right Revd Beilby Porteus (1731-1808), Lord Bishop of London.

CHAPTER 16

MAJOR = Here, grown-up, that is, twenty-one years of age or older.

LORD ELDON = The first Earl (1751-1838) was Lord Chancellor from 1801 till 1827. Everyone remembered that he eloped (ran away to get married) in 1772.

TILBURY = A light, two-wheeled carriage without a boot or top, named after its inventor, a London coachbuilder. It was popular in the first half of the nineteenth century, introduced c 1820, with a rib-backed seat, and mounted on six springs.

OMPHALE = A queen of Lydia (now almost the whole of that portion of Turkey immediately north of the island of Rhodes, $36.5°N$, $28°E$), to whom Hercules was sold as a slave for three years, as punishment for slaying Iphitus.

CLIPPERS = What we should now call 'fast movers'. Clipper originally meant, 'one who clips coin'; but became the slang-word for anything or anyone of high quality. Eric Partridge tells us that the word was coined in USA c 1835, and reached Britain c 1845; in which case it is an anachronism.

DIMITY = Stout cotton cloth, woven with raised stripes and fancy figures, used undyed for beds [Greek Di-, 'double' + Mitos, 'thread'].

TWILLED = Having parallel, diagonal ridges [Low German Twillen, 'to make double'].

MAIL = Mail-coach, which took passengers as well as mail.

CLANDESTINE = Secret (from Clam, in the original sense of Clamp; an instrument for holding fast: whence 'clam up' for a refusal to divulge information).

PROFLIGATE = Originally 'struck down' or 'ruined', it came to mean 'wicked; given up to vice' [Latin Profligātus].

ENSCONCED = Settled down; entrenched [probably from Latin Abscondere, 'to hide; conceal; shelter'].

DECAMPED = Took herself off; went away [opposite of 'made camp'].

SURREPTITIOUS = Secret in a rather shameful way; underhand [Latin Surripere, 'to pilfer'].

CHAPTER 17

MR GEORGE ROBINS = An auctioneer who died in 1847, when _Vanity Fair_ began to appear in monthly parts.

OBSEQUIES = The events which happen after a person dies (Mediaeval Latin _Obsequiae_, ´funeral rites´).

VERACIOUSLY = Truthfully (Latin V̄erācis, ´true´).

DISSIPATING = Squandering [Latin _Dissipāre_, ´to throw about´].

SHAMPOOING = Going through the motions of pressing and pulling; kneading the mattresses to assess their value.

DEPRECATE = Express disapproval of. It is possible that Mr Hammerdown does not mean this, but ´depreciate´ - ´talk about as if worth little´ (compare Latin D̄eprecāri, ´to pray against´, with D̄epretiāre, ´to lower the price´).

NANKEEN-JACKET = A jacket of cotton, usually yellow, formerly manufactured in Nanking, 350 miles south south-west of Peking, in China: 32°N, 118°C.

BANYHANN-TREE = Indian fig-tree whose branches grow out and then down to take root, so that eventually the tree covers a prodigious area (now spelt _Banyan_, from _Banian_, ´native Indian merchant´).

PAGODY = Sacred tower built over the relics of Buddha (Hindi _But-gadah_ from _But_, ´idol´ + _Gadah_, ´house´) usually written and pronounced _Pagoda_.

SQUARE PIANO = In fact, rectangular, with the strings horizontal from side to side (as the majority of pianos had till the end of the _nineteen_th century).

BABY-HOUSES = Dolls´ houses.

CURRICLE = Light, two-wheeled carriage drawn by two horses abreast (Latin _Currere_, ´to run´; ´a run-about´).

SECLUDED WIFE = Stay-at-home wife (Latin S̄eclūdere ´to shut away´).

BROUGHAM (pronounced ´broom´) = One-horse closed carriage with two or originally four wheels to carry two or four people (after the first Lord Brougham & Vaux, 1778-1868), introduced c 1838.

CUTTING A FLY OFF THE HORSE´S EAR - with his whip.

CHAPTER 18

MARCH, ANNO DOMINI 1815 = The background of the incidents we are about to read is this: Napoleon had made an ally of the Tsar (the ruler of Russia, whose title meaning Caesar (as did the German <u>Kaiser</u>) was later spelt Czar), but alienated him - lost him as an ally - by marrying an Austrian princess, and denying the Tsar freedom of action in Turkey. When he found that Napoleon's blockade (in which he himself had joined) was hurting his own people, the Tsar opened Russian ports to the British.

Napoleon invaded Russia, but was defeated by the winter cold, and an Allied army defeated him at Leipzig (which Thackeray spells Leipsic) in 1813. Napoleon abdicated, and was banished to the island of Elba (to the south of Tuscany: 43°N, 10°E); but he returned to France when he learned of dissension among the Allies at Vienna. His entry to Paris was a triumph, and he sat on the imperial throne once more.

You will read in coming chapters how the Allies defeated Napoleon at Waterloo, a Belgian village 50.7° north, and 4.4° east: ten miles south of Brussels: after his success against the Prussians under Blücher, and Marshal Ney's defeat by the Duke of Wellington at Quatre Bras, in 1815.

Again, Napoleon abdicated, in favour of his son, and tried to escape to America; but Captain Maitland, RN, captured him on HMS 'Bellerophon', and he was banished in 1816 to the island of St Helena (in the south Atlantic ocean; some 16° south, 8° west; nearer Africa than South America), where he died in 1821.

HIS BILLS WERE PROTESTED = His money-orders were formally refused.

'WHY DO YOU SHRINK FROM PLUNGING INTO THE GAZETTE?' = To be 'in the Gazette' meant to be published - and therefore known to everybody - as a bankrupt (and therefore not permitted to borrow money or write cheques).

VILIPENDING = Talking about as worthless (Latin <u>Vilipendere</u>, 'to hold in slight esteem').

JEOPARDISED = Put at risk (Late Latin <u>Jocus partitus</u>, 'game as easily lost as won').

CHASSE A L'AIGLE = Eagle-hunt (the eagle being Napoleon) (French).

GAZETTED TO HIS COMPANY = Announced in the London Gazette as posted, or appointed.

EPAULETS = Shoulder-pieces (ornamental badges worn on the shoulders of their coats by officers) (French).

BUXOM = Bright and jolly (originally 'tractable; obliging'; from Anglo-Saxon Buhsom, 'compliant; obedient').

CHAPTER 19

ALEXIS SOYER = The most famous chef of his day (1809-1858); he fled from France to London in 1830, and was chef at the Reform Club from 1837 to 1850.

COLLINGWOOD = Admiral Lord Collingwood (1750-1810) hoped to perpetuate the supply of wood for sailing ships in this way.

SHE HAD THE STREET LAID KNEE-DEEP WITH STRAW = A step taken when important people were ill, because it lessened the noise of cart and carriage wheels, and of horses´ hooves.

THE KNOCKER PUT BY = The door-knocker temporarily taken off.

DRAUGHTS = Doses of medicine (Middle English Draht, ´quantity of liquid drunk at once´ - at one gulp).

HYGIEIA = The Greek goddess of health.

EPICURES = ´Those who cultivate a refined taste for the pleasures of the table´ [the Greek philosopher Epicurus taught that pleasure was the supreme good, and pain the worst evil, in human life].

DIVISIONS = The separating of Members of Parliament into two groups, so that their votes can be counted.

MOTLEY = The dress of court jesters (Thackeray´s idea is that it is no fun having to make people laugh).

INVEIGLED = Enticed [originally, ´to blind in judgement´; from Latin Ab-, ´without´ + Oculus, ´an eye´].

PERDITION = Utter destruction [Latin Perdere, ´to destroy, squander, kill, lose or forget´].

IMMOLATING = Sacrificing [Latin Im-, ´on´ + Mola, ´meal´ - meal (or grain ground into powder); the point being that beasts which were to be sacrificed were first sprinkled with meal].

EMISSARIES = Here, messengers; people sent to negotiate privately [Latin Emissārius, 'A spy or scout', in the sense of someone sent ahead of an army to spy out the land].

SPUNGING-HOUSE = A preliminary place of confinement for debtors; where people arrested for debt were kept for 24 hours, to give their families and friends an opportunity of settling the debt [so-called because of the extortionate charges made by the bailiff for providing bed and board - he sponged on them].

NABOB = The deputy-governor (or any big-wig) [Hindi Nawwab].

MISANTHROPES = Haters of the human race [Greek Mise-ein, 'to hate' + Anthropos, 'man'].

QUACKS = Charlatans; pretenders to medical knowledge [so-called because they would 'cry their wares' at fairs or markets].

BAILIFFS = Court officers; here, rent collectors [Latin Bājulīvus, 'steward; manager'].

DUNS = People demanding payment of debts.

BLAND = Soothing [Latin Blandus, 'soft; agreeable; caressing'].

PHARMACOPOEIA = A book listing medicines, with instructions for their preparation and use [Greek Pharmakon, 'medicine' + Poie-ein, to make'].

HARPY = Monster (of a particular kind, with the face of a woman, and the claws and wings of a bird, which legend supposed to prey on men) [Greek Harpuiai, 'snatchers'].

STANHOPE = A light, open, originally one-seated vehicle, first made in 1816 with two wheels for The Revd The Honourable Fitzroy Stanhope (1787-1864), but later made with four. The gig (two-wheeled version) was hung on four springs, and had a rib-backed driving seat.

CUT = Pretended not to know (an almost unbelievably hurtful manoeuvre).

CHAPTER 20

BALKED = Here, deprived; disappointed [Anglo-Saxon Balca, ´a ridge or beam´; hence, to balk is to bar the way of someone].

ESTHER = See the book of that name in the Holy Bible, chapter 2. Pronounced ESTA.

WAN = Pale [Anglo-Saxon Wann, ´Dark; dusky´; hence, colourless].

HYMENEAL = concerning a wedding [Greek Humenaios, ´pertaining to marriage´].

FLORID = Rosy; red-faced [Latin Floridus, ´flowery; blooming; gay´].

BLEAR-EYED = Sore, watery-eyed [Middle-English Blere, ´misty; dim´].

PUMPS = Here, shoes with thin soles and soft uppers; dancing-pumps [propably from the ´pomp´ of occasions when they were worn, for they were Court dress].

WAFERS = Small discs of flour mixed with gum, used for sealing letters, attaching papers, or receiving the impress of a seal [Dutch Wafel, ´a thin cake´].

BUMPERS = Full measures [French Bombard, ´cannon´; hence, a black jack (or black-leather liquor-jug) which looked like a miniature cannon].

SKULKING = Stealthy [Norwegian Skulka, ´to lurk´].

COLLUSION = Secret agreement to deceive [Latin Colludere, ´to act secretly´].

SENILE = Caused by old age [Latin Senilis, ´concerning old people´].

CONDOLES = Expresses sympathy (the thought is, expresses sympathy formally, because he thinks he ought to; and therefore without actually feeling sympathetic) [Latin Condolere, ´to feel pain´].

PRIG = Conceited fellow [from Prick, in the sense, ´to dress up´].

HANKERING = Here, hanging (in the intensive form, ´forever hanging´).

COLLOQUY = Talk together [Latin Colloquium, ´a speaking-together´].

37

RALLYING = Attacking in fun [French _Railler_, 'to chaff; to scoff at'].

THREE STARS TO HER NAME = Indicating that she held much stock (in effect, many shares in the company).

STREELED = Trailed along the ground.

PARAGON = Model or pattern of excellence [Old French].

MULATTO = Half European, half negro [as a MULE is the off-spring of a horse and an ass].

TALLOW TRADE = The business of melting down the fat of animals, and clarifying it to make candles [Middle English _Talgh_, 'animal fat'].

TURTLE-FED = In effect, in the habit of dining on luxury foods, as successful business men pride themselves on doing.

CHAPTER 21

DISINTERESTED = Here, unprejudiced; not out for their own advantage - not ´having an interest´ in the sense of turning things to their profit; strictly, impartial (a completely different word from <u>uninterested</u>, which means ´could not care less´).

WAG = anyone ludicrously mischievous [probably short for ´waghalter´ - ´likely to swing from the gallows´ and so ´wag´ while hanging from a ´halter´. Compare the Scottish word <u>Hempie</u>; which has come to mean ´a frolicsome fellow´, but literally means, ´one fit for the hempen rope´].

OBTUSE = Here, stupid; dull [Latin, meaning the opposite of ´sharp; acute´; <u>Obtūsus</u>, ´blunt; dull´].

ODIOUS = Deserving hatred [Latin <u>Odiōsus</u>, ´hateful; vexatious´].

TEMPORISED = ´Played for time´ [Latin <u>Tempus</u>, ´time´].

CONNED OVER = Discussed in a critical, analytical way [Old English <u>Con</u>, a variant of <u>Can</u>, ´to scan, to pore over; to examine; ´to learn´].

TAGS = Ornamental pendants [Swedish <u>Tagg</u>, ´a point´; akin to <u>Tack</u>, ´a small, short nail´].

GIMCRACKS = Knick-knacks [perhaps from slang <u>Gim</u>, ´neat; spruce´; + <u>Crack</u>, ´a boy´; hence, by turn, ´a neat-looking lad´; ´a neat piece of mechanism´; ´any neat trinket or toy´].

REVILING = Talking about her in an unpleasant, abusive way [Old French <u>Reviler</u>, from <u>Re-</u>, ´once more´ + <u>Vilis</u>, ´cheap; common; of no value´ - both Latin roots].

HOTTENTOT = A member of a degraded South African tribe [Dutch <u>Hot en tot</u>, ´Hot´ and ´tot´ are intended to imitate sounds frequent in the tribal language; in the way that the Greek word <u>Barbaros</u>, ´barbarian´, is an imitation of unintelligible speech].

VENUS = A beauty; as we should say, ´a glamour girl´ [from the Roman goddess of love and beauty].

CHAPTER 22

TATTOOED = Drummed his fingers [formerly <u>Taptoo</u>; the drum and bugle signal that soldiers must finish their drinks, and get back to barracks].

BANDANNA = Coloured [Hindi <u>Bandhnu</u>, ´tie-dyed´].

CURACOA = Liqueur made of spirits (or alcoholic drink made by distilling alcohol) flavoured with the peel of bitter oranges, cinnamon (the inner bark of a type of laurel tree grown in Ceylon) and mace (the powdered outer coat of nutmeg seed) and sweetened) [Curacoa is an island in the Caribbean sea, 12°N, 69°W].

HUMMUMS = Turkish baths [Arabid <u>Hammam</u>]. The meaning is not obvious, because an hotel and coffeehouse of this name stood till 1865 on the site of a former Turkish bath, at the south-west corner of Russell Street and Covent Garden.

TRAP = Two-wheeled open carriage [whose name refers to its trappings by way of decoration, horse-brasses, &c] such as phaeton, dog-cart, sulky, and so on, as opposed to a gentleman´s closed carriage.

JACKETS = That is, facing-bricks instead of the stone later used for facing them.

ACHILLES/PIMLICO ARCH/EQUESTRIAN MONSTER = The statue (1822), arch (1825) and statue of the Duke of Wellington (1846) which were erected to commemorate the battle of Waterloo.

GLASS COACHES = Originally, in the seventeenth century, coaches with glass windows; here, coaches from private firms which would be hired by arrangement, as opposed to those which plied for hire (rather the difference between the present-day hired limousine and taxi).

THE PAIR IN WHICH THE GENTLEMAN USED TO SHAVE HIMSELF = An advertisement for Warren´s blacking, in which a boot was used as a shaving mirror.

PELISSE = Here, an outdoor garment of ankle-length, with or without sleeves - to be seen in museums of costume, such as that in the Victoria & Albert Museum, or at Bath [French for a garment made or lined with skins: Latin <u>Pellis</u>, ´skin´].

CHANTILLY LACE = Silk bobbin lace - made of a coarse thread by bobbins, as opposed to needles - of great delicacy, made in the area of Chantilly, Bayeux, and surrounding districts: 49°N, 2.5°E.

GROOMSMAN = Best man, who attends the bridegroom [Old English Brȳd, ´a woman about to be married´ + Guma, ´a man´; hence, ´a man about to marry a bride´].

POSTILLIONS´ FAVOURS DRAGGLED = A postillion was a young man who rode the near horse of the leaders of four in a carriage; on a ride of any importance, there would be a postillion on each pair of horses, and outriders as well - purely for show. [Italian Postiglione, ´postboy´]. Favours were (i) a knot of ribbons; or (ii) a glove; or (iii), most probably, a cockade [French Cocarde; ´a rosette of leather, worn on the hat by gentlemen´s servants´]. Draggled means ´soiled by being drawn through mud or wet grass´; here, it must mean simply ´looking as though they had been drawn through wet grass´.

TIFFIN = Lunch.

BATHING-MACHINES = Huts on wheels, used for changing in privacy into bathing costumes (or swimsuits, as we call them now).

MASTER OMNIUM = The youngest of a family invented by Matthew Higgins (1810-1868) to vivify his letters and articles for the press, on social evils: he became popularly known as ´Jacob Omnium´.

SIX-POUNDER = The barrel of a cannon throwing shot weighing six pounds per ball.

LAZZARONI = Beggars; homeless wanderers [Italian].

HARLEQUIN´S JACKET = Parti-coloured (that is, coloured differently in different parts, in a very large check) worn by the pantomime character partnering Columbine; or, rather, mutely rivalling the clown in trying to win Columbine´s affection. Harlequin is supposed to be invisible to the clown and to the pantaloon (another pantomime character, of an old man in slippers) [Italian Arlecchino].

JOINVILLE = The Prince de Joinville (1818-1900) was a French sailor; third son of King Louis Philippe (1773-1850).

DON JUAN = The proverbially heartless lover in a Spanish story first dramatized by Gabriel Tellez (1571-1641), and later by Moliere, and by Mozart, and by Bernard Shaw.

OGLE = Amorous glance; a stare calculated to win at least the interest of a person of the opposite sex [akin to Low German, Oegeln ´to eye frequently´].

FROGS = Fastenings by loops on one side, over buttons on the other [Portugese Froco, ´coat-tag´].

LACQUERED MUSTACHIOS = Moustache-ends twirled to a point, and kept there by applying yellow varnish [Portugese Lacre; from the Persian Lak, ´an insect whose punctures of the banyan tree cause the secretion of a resin used in varnishes´].

DUN = Debt collector.

BAILIFF = Court officer likely to take away goods if debts were left unpaid.

PIQUET = Card-game for two, using 32 cards excluding the number 2-6 [French Pique, ´pike´ or ´lance´; a spade at cards - the ace of spades being the highest card].

CHAPTER 23

DR ELLIOTSON = John Elliotson (1791-1868); professor of medicine at London University from 1831, and founder of University College. He founded the Phrenological Society, did research in pharmacology, was one of the first to use a stethoscope, aand was deprived of his professorial chair in 1838 because he advocated hypnosis. He published <u>Numerous Cases of Surgical Operation without Pain in the Mesmeric State</u> in 1843.

CHIMNEY-GLASS = Mirror over the fireplace.

PLENIPOTENTIARY = Someone given full powers to act on behalf of someone else [Latin <u>Plenus</u>, ´full´ + <u>Potens</u>, ´powerful´].

MACHIAVELLIAN = Cunning [Niccolo di Bernado dei Machiavelli (1469-1527) was an Italian statesman with a not-altogether-deserved reputation for being wickedly cunning].

ROUTS = Fashionable gatherings [Anglo-French <u>Rute</u>, ´a division or detachment of troops´; eventually, ´gatherings where the officers of such a division and their ladies might be met´].

CHAPTER 24

TAWNY = Brownish-yellow [Anglo-French <u>Taune</u>].

HUME & SMOLLETT = <u>History of England</u> written from 1754 to 1726 by David Hume (1711-76), continued by Tobias George Smollett (1721-71) published in 1793).

CELLAR-BOOK = Notebook listing all the wines stored, bought and drunk.

ESCRITOIRE = Writing-desk [French <u>Écritoire</u>].

LIVID = Blue-grey [Latin <u>Lividus</u>, ´blue-black´].

DEPÔT = Headquarters [French <u>Dépôt</u>].

LEVEE = Afternoon assembly at which the Sovereign or his representative receives only men [French <u>Levé</u>].

AFFAIRE LA = Domestic affairs; personal arrangements [to make].

<u>ROBE DE CHAMBRE</u> = Smoking jacket (the smell of cigars or pipes clings to the clothes of the smoker; for which reason smokers wore jackets when they smoked which were not worn at other times) or dressing-gown.

<u>POULET</u> = Amorous or playful letter to a member of the opposite sex.

<u>QUE VOULEZ VOUS</u>? = In effect, ´What do you expect?´

PEREGRINATIONS = Rounds; wanderings-about [Latin <u>Peregrīnarī</u> ´to travel (in foreign countries)´].

ACCOUTREMENT-MAKER´S = One who makes and sells personal equipment other than clothing [French <u>Accoutrement</u>, ´equipment´].

LIGHT BOBS = Light infantry (foot-soldiers: the Italian word <u>Infante</u> means ´a youth´, or ´a foot-soldier´ - because older men cannot usually walk far).

HACKNEY-COACH = A four-wheeled coach (usually, a town-coach discarded by a nobleman) with seats for six passengers, drawn by two horses, plying for hire (that is, going about the streets empty till a would-be passenger signalled to the

driver) [Old French <u>Haquenée</u>, 'an ambling horse', as opposed to a hunter, which
would be expected to jump fences]:   succeeded c 1835 by the four-wheeled cab, or
'growler'.

CAJOLERIES = Coaxings [Old French Cageoler, ´to sing or twitter like a bird in a cage´. The French verb actually contains the noun ´cage´].

NINCOMPOOP = Simpleton; fool [Latin Non compos mentis, ´not of sound mind´]. There is another meaning in the Dictionary of the Vulgar Tongue, 1811.

PITTANCE = Small sum of money [Old French Pitance, ´pity´; in other words, a gift of charity (and therefore as small as the giver´s conscience would allow him to give)].

ECARTE = Game for two in which cards of value 2 to 6 are excluded, and players may discard any of (or all) the cards dealt, and replace them from the pack [French Ecarter, ´to discard´].

DISTINGUEE = Distinguished.

ENNUI = Weariness; want of interest in one´s surroundings [French Anui, ´annoy´; Latin In odio, ´in disgust or hatred´].

BACKGAMMON = Game on a board consisting of two tables hinged together, with draughtsmen moving at throws of the dice (so named because the draughtsmen are often obliged to go back).

FLY = One-horse covered carriage originally pulled by men; introduced at Brighton in 1816, it was a landaulet (a small landau - carriage made in 1743 at the town in Rheinland-Pfalz, 50 miles south of Mainz, and east of Saarbrucken).

PAS = The right to go first (in this instance, the merit to deserve being recounted - described - first).

NAIVETE = Simplicity; unaffectedness; naturalness: in a delicate and old-fashioned sense of the word, ´silliness´: pronounced ´Nigh-eve-té´.

TERMAGANT = Over-bearing person [originally, an imaginary deity thought by Christians to be worshipped by Mohammedans].

CHAPERON = A married woman accompanying a young unmarried woman in public as a protector [French, ´hood´; perhaps in the sense that Mohammedan women wear a veil for protection].

CONFIDANTE = A person entrusted with secrets [Latin <u>Confīdere</u>, ´to have full trust´].

BENEFACTRESS = Woman who has done one a good turn, or promoted one´s well-being [Latin <u>Bene</u>, ´well´ + <u>Facere</u>, ´to do´].

MACHINATIONS = Schemes; plots [Latin <u>Māchina</u>; in this sense, ´a stratagem or trick´].

HARPIES = Monsters with the heads and bodies of women, but the wings and claws of birds [Greek <u>Harpuiai</u>, ´the snatchers´].

PULING = Whining [French <u>Piauler</u>, ´to whine´].

DRAGOON = Cavalryman [certain regiments of cavalry were called dragoons, but the reason for the name is not entirely clear: it has to do with their muskets, but there is disagreement as to whether i', was because of the shape of the butt, or the fact that, like the dragon, they breathed fire].

SPINSTER = The legal name for an unmarried woman ranking from a viscount´s daughter downwards [a very ancient word arising from the fact that almost all unmarried women spun thread on a spinning wheel, where married women tended their children, or prepared food].

CHAPTER 26

BAROUCHE = A four-wheeled carriage with a seat outside for the driver, and seats inside for two couples facing each other, with a calash top - a kind of hood - over the rear seat [German Barutsche; Latin Bis, ´double´ + Rota ´wheel´].

CALIPASH = The part of a turtle next to the upper shell, not unlike green gelatine [a form of Calabash, meaning Carapace, ´upper shell´; from Portuguese Calabaca (Arabic Qar, ´gourd´ + Aibas, ´dry´)].

CALIPEE = The part of a turtle next to the lower shell, and yellow in colour.

THE EMPEROR HALIXANDER´S SISTER = The Emperor and the Grand Duchess of Oldenburgh (latitude 53.5°N; longitude 8°E).

WALK ALONG THE FLAGS = Walk along the stones of the path [Old Norse Flaga, ´a slab of stone´].

ULTRA-MATERNAL = Very, very motherly [Latin Ultra-, ´beyond´].

VALET = A man´s personal servant, who attends to his clothing, &c [Old French Vaslet, ´A little vassal´, or ´retainer´; again, a personal servant].

SUPERCILIOUS = Haughty; contemptuous: literally, ´with eyebrows raised´ [Latin Super, ´above´ + Cilium, ´eyelid´].

EBULLITION = Bubbling-over [Latin Ēbullīre, ´to bubble up´].

MUFFIN = A soft, round, spongy cake (probably from the word Muff, because of its softness).

BANEFUL = Sinister; disquieting [literally, ´murderous´; from the Anglo-Saxon Bana, ´murderer; destroyer´].

DAMASK = Rich, silk, figured fabric; or twilled - ribbed, by doubling certain warp-threads - linen, originally made at Damascus.

PAVILION = Literally, a tent on posts; here, a four-poster bed, with curtains round it, from the days when people had to go through one bedroom to reach another, and the curtains gave privacy to those whose bedroom was used as a passageway [French Pavillon; Latin Papilio, ´butterfly´ - because the tent-walls/bed-curtains resembled a butterfly´s wings].

OBDURATE = Stubborn;   hard-hearted [Latin <u>Ob</u>-, ´completely´ + <u>Dūrāre</u>, ´to harden;].

PARAGON = Example of excellence;   a model of all one should be [Latin <u>Para con</u>, ´compared with´].

MOLLIFYING = Softening [Latin <u>Mollis</u>, ´soft´ + <u>Facere</u>, ´to make´].

CARTE BLANCHE = Complete freedom to decide [French for ´white paper´, signed in consent to terms to be filled in by the bearer].

PACKETS = Mail-boats (short for ´mail-packet boats´).

<u>PEKIN</u> = Civilian (a contemptuous word for men who were not in uniform, coined by Napoleon´s soldiers).

DRAFT = Money-order [early Middle English <u>Draht</u>, not found in Old English;   from common Teutonic <u>Dragan</u>, ´to draw´].

QUIZ = Enquirer;   asker of puzzling questions.

DEMURE = Serious;   dignified, with the idea of affectation, as though the person could not be quite so serious and devoted to duty as he or she looked [an extended form of the Middle English <u>Mure</u>, ´calm;   grown-up´].

CHAPTER 27

SHELLS = Shoulder-pieces, which neeed some explaining. The sign of an officer was his epaulets; which, being made of ´bullion´ (gold or silver-thread), were very expensive. On an undress-coat (a coat not intended to be worn on the most important occasions), therefore, he would wear small brass plates instead, known as shells [French Ecailles, ´scales´ - shaped not unlike fish-scales, but bigger].

WEDDING-PELISSE = Wedding gown.

QUADRILLE = A dance in five movements, by four couples who each form the side of a square [Latin Quadra, ´square´].

BILLET = Short note [a billet is a little bill, from the Latin Bulla, ´seal´ - hence, ´document´].

FIST = Slang word for ´writing´; handwriting.

TAY-BOY = Tea-boy, said with an Irish accent.

BATTERY = A number of cannon, or huge guns, which would batter whatever they fired at.

WALCHEREN AGUE = A disease caught on the Dutch island at the mouth of the river Shelde [latitude 51.5^{o}N, longitude 3°E].

LOO = Originally, Lanter-loo; a game of cards played with three cards (at first, with five), whose name comes from the meaningless refrain of a popular song of long ago.

USURPER = A person who takes someone else´s place with no right to it [Latin Usurpāre, ´to displace another wrongly´].

NEGUS = A drink made of wine, hot water, sugar, nutmeg and lemon juice, said to have been invented by Colonel Francis Negus (who served under the Duke of Marlborough, and died in 1732).

TRANSPORTS = Ships employed by the Government for carrying soldiers and military stores [Latin Trans-, ´across´ + Portāre, ´to carry´].

CHAPTER 28

ASSIDUITY = Perseverance [Latin Assidēre, 'to sit down to (something)'].

FORAGING CAP = Type of hat worn by soldiers sent out to forage (that is, look for food), and worn on the side of the head, where it would not be knocked off - as an ordinary hat would - by sacks, and so forth, carried on the shoulder; later called a forage cap [French Fourrage, from Old French Feurre, 'fodder'].

DUCK TROUSERS = Trousers of coarse cloth [Dutch Doek, 'cloth'].

COMMISSARY-GENERAL = Head of the department responsible for supplying the army with transport, camp equipment, and food and drink [Mediaeval Latin Commisārius].

COURIER = Messenger [Mediaeval Latin Currerius, 'a professional runner', from Currere, 'to run'].

MENIAL = Domestic servant (ultimately from Late Latin Masnata; the origin of Mansion, 'household'].

'PAS SI BÊTE' = 'Tell me another'; or, 'Ask me another' [in other words, 'Don't be so silly'].

CHAUSSEES = Causeways, or paved roads [Latin Calciata via, 'paved way' or, as we say now, 'made-up road'].

EQUIPAGES = Here, carriages and horses [Old Norse Skipa, 'to man (a ship)'].

CHÂTEAUX = Castles [Latin Castella, 'little fortresses'].

MR GLEIG'S 'STORY OF THE BATTLE OF WATERLOO' = Thackeray's source of information and 'constant companion' while he was writing the chapters about the battle. George Robert Gleig (1796-1888) was son of the Bishop of Brechin: he studied at Glasgow University and at Balliol College, Oxford; became Chaplain General (1844) and Inspector General of military schools (1846).

PRISTINE = Initial [Latin Pristinus, 'former; just past; ancient'].

'REPAYTHER' = Repeater; a watch which strikes the hours if its spring is pressed.

GAZABO = Gazebo; a look-out tower [the name is said to have been formed on the model of the Latin word, <u>Videbo</u>, ´I shall see´; but it may come from an oriental word so far untraced].

AUGUST JOBBERS = Important people who turn a public undertaking to private advantage.

GOURMAND = Glutton; ´greedy pig´ [French; a different word from <u>Gourmet</u>, ´a connoisseur of table delicacies´].

CATALANI = Angelica Catalani (1779-1849) was a famous singer, whose ´voice was so full, powerful and clear: her intonation so pure and true, and her instinctive execution of difficult and brilliant music so easy and unfaltering: that her singing had a charm which has scarcely ever been equalled´ (<u>Grove´s Dictionary of Music and Musicians</u>, 1927).

JAUNT = Pleasure trip.

JUNKET = Private entertainment or banquet [Old Norman French <u>Jonquette</u>, ´rush basket´ - in which cream cheese was kept].

PRECIPITANCY = Haste [Latin <u>Praecipitis</u>, ´headlong´].

STAYS = Waistcoat stiffened with whalebone to look particularly smart.

BROUGHAMS = One-horse closed carriages [after the first Lord Brougham & Vaux who commissioned the first from Sharp & Bland of South Audley Street in 1830 (but found it too heavy, and got a much improved version from Robinson & Cook of Mount Street)].

GARNERS = Gardeners.

CHAPTER 29

CATTLE = Horses, or cows, or sheep, or goats, or mules, or asses, or even camels [from Late Latin Capitāle, ´property´]; here, ´the pair of horses´.

ARAB = Arabian pony.

AIDE-DE-CAMP = Field-assistant; an officer who receives and passes on the orders of a General.

SQUADRON = The principal division of a regiment of cavalry (´soldiers on horseback´); the ´little troop of horsemen´ mentioned in paragraph one.

TOILETTES = Here, modes of dress; styles of clothing.

CAIRNGORMS = Brooches made of yellow or brown rock-crystal found in the Cairngorm mountains of Scotland.

COUP-D´OEIL = Sight; view [French].

STOCK = Cravat; band of cloth worn round the neck.

LOGE = Box at the theatre; loggia (a gallery running along part of the circle, open to the stage, and divided on that side by a series of slender pillars) [Italian, ´Lodge or porch´].

LOBBY = Entrance hall [Late Latin Lobia, ´arbour or portico´].

SCREW = Miser (presumably the source of the name of Dickens´s character, Scrooge).

L----- OSBORNES = Osborne was the family name of the Dukes of Leeds.

OPERA-GLASS = Small telescope.

LORGNON = Binoculars, as we should call them [French Lorgner, ´to keep an eye on; to watch; to make eyes at´].

COMPOSITOR = Type-setter.

AMBROSIAL = Heavenly [Green A-, ´not + (M)Brotos, ´mortal´].

APPARITION = Appearance [Latin Ad-, ´to´ + Parere,, to show oneself´].

DRAGON = Perhaps a pun, because it can mean either a fierce, violent person or a dragoon: Thackeray might well mean both simultaneously, referring to the General.

GREEN = Inexperienced; easily imposed on (as a twig is easily bent when it is young and green).

DARIUS = Between 548 BC and 330 BC, there were three warring kings of Persia named Darius. Probably, the first is meant.

A NOBLE DUCHESS = The Duchess of Richmond gave just such a ball.

DEBUT = Entrance into society.

DISTINGUE = Well-bred.

CHAUSSEE = Shod - how she could wear such shoes.

CORSETIERE = Corset-maker.

JARGON = Talk; way of putting things into words [Old French, ´the twittering of birds; meaningless chatter´].

TRES AIMABLE = Very kind.

NOSEGAY = Little bunch of flowers.

BUMPERS = Glasses full.

´LIGHT UP YOUR LANTERN JAWS´ = ´Cheer up your long, thin face´.

SAMBRE = River in northern France eventually flowing into the Meuse: 50.5°N, 5°E.

SUPERSCRIPTION = Address on the envelope.

CHAPTER 30

CURL PAPERS = Pieces of paper round which women would curl their hair, leaving the papers till the curls had stiffened.

CAMISOLE = A short-sleeved bodice of white cloth, worn over stays to protect the dress worn on top; sometimes called a waistcoat [French, ´a little camise´ - Late Latin Camisa, ´shirt´].

VALISE = Case [French, ´travelling bag´].

HABILIMENTS = Garments [Latin Habilis, ´suitable; fitting´].

KNAPSACK = A bag carried on the shoulders [Low German Knap-, ´to nibble´].

EQUANIMITY = Evenness of temper; calmness [Latin Aequus, ´level´ + Animus, ´mind; soul´].

CORSAGE = Bodice; the part of a dress which covers the ribs [French].

CASHMERE SHAWLS = Fine, costly shawls made of the soft downy wool of goats, at Kashmir in India: 33°N, 77°E.

BIJOU = Trinket [Breton Bizou, ´a ring with a stone´, from Biz, ´finger´].

ODIOUS = Hateful [Latin Odiōsus].

EGOTISM = Self-Love; self-centredness [Latin Ego, ´I´].

BILLETS = Lodgings [Anglo-Latin Billetta, ´a little note´ - in this case, an order to accommodate a soldier or soldiers; hence, the house where soldiers are accommodated].

BRAVOS = ´Daring fellows´; the Italian and Spanish equivalent of a Red Indian brave, or warrior.

BARDS = Poets [Celtic].

CHAPTER 31

<u>BONNE</u> = Servant-girl.

<u>TRENCHANT</u> = Incisive; penetrating [Old French <u>Trencher</u>, ´to cut´].

<u>TARTINES</u> = Slices of bread, butter and jam.

<u>DISCOMFITURE</u> = Defeat [Latin <u>Dis-</u>, ´the undoing or opposite of´ + <u>Conficere</u>, ´to put together´; in other words, ´to fall apart´].

<u>FROGGED</u> = Fastening by buttons or tags on one side through loops on the other (the ´frog´ is the tag or large button) [Portuguese <u>Froco</u>].

<u>CORBLEU!</u> = ´By Jove´.

<u>ALLÉE VERTE</u> = Green Avenue (the English word Alley, from the French <u>Aller</u>, ´to go´, means ´a walk´, or ´a road along which people like to walk´).

FARO = Belgian beer.

´<u>TENEZ</u>, <u>MADAME</u>, <u>EST-CE QU´IL N´EST PAS AUSSI A L´ARMÉE</u>, <u>MON HOMME A MOI</u>? = ´Look here, ma´am; isn´t my man off to the army too?´

<u>MAITRE D´HÔTEL</u> = Butler.

HULKS = Old ships used as prisons.

BRAVES = Lads (think of Red Indian braves); warriors.

PONTOONS = Prison-ships (another reference to the hulks).

QUARTER = Mercy; clemency (because one assigned living-quarters to prisoners allowed to live).

SIRRAH! = Fellow! [The word ´sir´ said with anger, or with contemptuous force].

MORTIFIED = Wounded (in his pride) [fashionable exaggeration of one´s feelings - ´I nearly died´ - in that to mortify is to cause to die, from Latin <u>Mortificāre</u>, ´to do to death´].

CURRICLE = Two-wheeled vehicle drawn by two horses abreast [Latin Currĕre, ´to run], hooded and low-slung, made popular by the Prince Regent (later George IV).

AVOWAL = A declaration (of love) [Latin Advocāre, ´to summon as a witness´].

MUSTACHIOS = Moustaches; except that Thackeray´s spelling brings out the inner meaning more [Greek Mustax, ´mouth-touchers´].

C´EST LE FEU! = ´That´s gun-fire´.

CHAPTER 32

CHAUSSEE = Causeway; paved road [Latin Calciāre, ´to shoe´, led to Calciāta Via, ´paved way´; or, as we now say, ´made-up road´].

SON HOMME A ELLE = Her man; her sweetheart.

BON VOYAGE = ´A pleasant journey to you´; as we should say now, ´Happy travelling´, or, ´Good trip´.

PAS DE CHEVAUX, SACREBLEU! = ´No horses, confound it!´.

HUSSAR = Light cavalryman (originally, Hungarian cavalryman - during the wars against the Turks, every husz [´twenty´] families had to provide one cavalryman).

SABRE = Here, cavalry sword [French; altered from Sable].

LEONORA = In the poem Lenore, by Gottfried Burger of Gottingen in Lower Saxony, the heroine is carried away on horseback by a spectre.

DEBACLE = Collapse [from Latin De-, ´undoing´ + Baculus, ´a bar or barrier´; as when ice melts in the hitherto frozen river].

FLAGON = Large bottle [Latin Flasco, ´flask´].

MA BONNE PETITE DAME = ´My kind little lady´.

CONSOLE-TABLE = Table whose leaf is supported by a bracket at each end.

COQUET = To preen like a cock strutting before hens.

COUPEZ-MOI = ´Shave me´; VITE = ´Quickly´.

COUPY = ´Cut´; RASY = ´Shave´.

NE PORTY PLOO = ´Don´t carry more´.

[Thackeray spells these phrases as they sound, to emphasize that Jos does not fully understand what he is saying.]

BONNY A VOO = ´A cap for you´.

PRENNY DEHORS = 'Take [them] outside'.

VENNY MAINTENONG = 'Come now'.

SWEEVY 'After [me]'; ALLY = 'Go'; PARTY = 'Be off'; DONG LA ROO = 'Into the street'.

PORTE-COCHERE = Gateway; main entrance.

IMPERIALS = Bags.

FEMME DE CHAMBRE = Maid.

BAILIFFS = Stewards [Latin Bājulīvus, 'manager'].

SACKS = Lootings (because loot is carried in a sack).

PAROXYSM = Climax (Greek, 'sharp excess').

CASE-BOTTLE = Bottle made to fit into a case with others; often rectangular.

DISAFFECTED = Unfriendly; alienated.

LOUIS, THE DESIRED = Louis XVIII (1755-1824) was sometimes referred to as Louis le Desire.

PORTMANTEAU = Trunk [designed to porte, 'carry', one's manteau, or 'mantle'; one's cloak].

ABDUCTION = Being taken away [Latin Ab-, 'away' + Dūcere, 'to lead'].

COXCOMB = Superficial pretender to knowledge (the word refers to the cock's comb which was a jester's head-dress).

IN THE CABIN OF A CALM = 'During a time of quiet and tranquillity'.

CHAPTER 33

DAME DE COMPAGNIE = Paid companion.

DISCOMFITED = Over-thrown [Latin, ´fallen apart´].

FEMMME DE CHAMBRE = Lady´s maid (a superior servant).

BURTHEN = Burden; load (Anglo-Saxon Byrthen).

PALSIED = Short for ´paralysed´; disabled [Greek Para-, ´Aside´ + Luein, ´to loose´].

BENIGHTED = Kept in darkness.

SQUARETOES = Slang for a precise, formal, old-fashioned person.

GUINEA-FOWLS = Small fowl of the same order as peacocks and pheasants (that is, table delicacies).

DEMISE = Death [Latin, ´sent away´].

POST-OBITS = Bonds issued on the security of an expected legacy.

CURACOA = Liqueur flavoured with orange-peel, cinnamon (the inner bark of a tree of the laurel family) and mace (the dried husk of nutmeg-seed), sweetened, from the Caribbean island, 12°N, 69°W.

THE ALBANY = Now known as Albany: a suite of residential chambers for men near Piccadilly; plainly, as enviably fashionable then as now.

ATTACHÉ = One appointed to a certain level on the staff of an ambassador.

MACHIAVELLIAN = Scheming.

PRETENDU = Intended husband [French].

PROSELYTISER = One who makes converts [Greek Proselutos, ´having come´; that is, arrived at a particular position, so that one has a particular view of life - to which one was converted from another view].

RECUSANT = One who refuses to comply, or agree with the views of another [Latin Re-, ´against´ + Causa, ´the cause´; hence, Recūsans, ´making objection´].

TAKING DOWN THE BOLUS = Swallowing the mouthful - we often say of ideas we find unpalatable, ´That is a bit of a mouthful´; meaning, ´That is a more than I can swallow´ [The Latin word Bolus has several meanings, but its most usual meaning is that of the food-mass ready for swallowing which results from the work of our teeth and tongue in the seconds after we have taken a mouthful of food].

TEMPORIZE = To humour with a view to gaining time [Latin Tempus, Temporis, ´time´].

LOZENGE = Diamond-shaped panel with a coat of arms.

THREE LAMBS TROTTANT ARGENT, &c = A humorous version of heraldic language, describing the Southdown coat of arms (´Three silver lambs trotting´, and so on´).

COGNIZANCE = Badge or emblem [Latin Cognoscere, ´to know´; hence, a sign by which one can be known or recognized].

TRACTS = Pamphlets [an abbreviation of the Latin word Tractātus; a treatise, or book dealing with a particular subject].

CHAPTER 34

CARDS = Calling cards, which were left with the footman of families on whom distinguished people wished to call, before they actually paid them a visit. Such cards set out the name and address of the person wishing to visit, and are still sometimes left by callers who find that no one is in.

REPUBLICAN MISS CRAWLEY = The phrase is humorous, for Miss Crawley did not in the least favour a state in which people were equal. She liked feeling that others were much less important than she was.

DISSIPATION = Reckless pursuit of pleasure [Latin Dis-, ´away´ + Sipāre, ´to throw´].

NOTHING LOTH = Not unwilling (Old English Lath, ´hostile´].

ENGOUMENT = Infatuation; foolish doting; excessive fondness [French].

MADEIRA = Rich wine from the island of Madeira off north-west Africa: 33°N, 17°W.

LIAISON = Union; association [French].

PIQUET = Card-game for two, using cards worth more than six [French Pique, a spade at cards].

ARTIFICES = Wiles; crafty tricks [Latin Ars, ´art´ + Ficium, ´making´].

ODIOUS = Hateful [Latin Ōdisse, ´to hate´].

PARSIMONIOUS = Unduly careful with money; mean [Latin Parcere. ´to be careful´].

SCREW = Miser [Slang; Ebenezer Scrooge´s surname emodies the word, which pictures someone exacting the last drop of wealth from another].

SCREWED = Hard put to it to get by; hard-pressed [Old French Escrou, ´nut´, as twisted on a bolt].

SPOONEY = Silly fellow [slang for ´spoon-fed baby´].

PLUCKED = Failed [slang for 'pulled out of the bunch who were passed'].

STROKE = The oar whose user sits nearest the stern, the others taking their time from his 'stroke', or pace of rowing.

BACKBOARD = Doing exercises with a short plank attached to their spines to keep their backs straight.

COLLOQUY = Talk together [Latin Colloqui].

PORTMANTEAU = Travelling bag [French Porte, 'carries' + Manteau, 'mantle; cloak'].

PRETERNATURAL = Surpassing anything found in nature [Latin].

HOBBADEHOY = Hobbledehoy; clumsy or awkward youth.

FAST = Devoted to pleasure [slang], and hence neglectful of duty.

RUSTICATED = Sent home in disgrace [Latin Rus, 'the countryside' - where it was assumed that everyone would live if he were not at university].

FICKLE = Changeable; undependable [Old English Ficol, 'deceitful']: the idea is that a fickle person is too ready to behave as though friendly, when not moved by genuinely friendly feelings. In consequence, the promises or statements made while putting on this deceptively friendly manner cannot be relied on.

WHIPPERSNAPPER = 'One who does nothing but snap' - or crack - 'his whip'; a fidget; a nobody [slang].

VOLLEY = Burst (of laughter) [from the Latin Volāre, 'to let fly].

TETBURY PET/ROTTINGDEAN FIBBER = The names under which these bare-knuckles boxers fought.

SENIOR WRANGLER = A Cambridge graduate with First Class Honours in mathematics.

TAX-CART = Open two-wheeled cart, drawn by one horse, and used for agriculture or trade (therefore liable to tax at a reduced rate).

LITTLE-GO = Matriculation (entrance examination) at Cambridge.

PROCTORS = Officers responsible for college discipline.

LIBERTY HALL = An imaginary place where people can do what they please.

BUZZ = Finish to the last drop [slang].

GAMMON = An exclamation of disbelief, not unlike 'Rubbish!' [slang].

BLANDNESS = Smoothness [Latin Blandus, 'soft'].

PATRICIAN = Noble [Latin Patres, 'fathers' or senators of ancient Rome].

PUNCH = Long drink made of hot water, spirits, sugar, lemon juice and spice [Hindi Panch, 'five'; from the number of ingredients].

DRAG = Long, open stage-coach with four horses, and seats round the sides [Anglo-Saxon Dragan, 'to draw'].

VINOUS = Affected by the consumption of wine [Latin Vīnum, ´wine´].

IN VINO VERITAS = ´Truth comes out in wine´ [the Roman author, Pliny].

MARS, BACCHUS, APOLLO VIRORUM = Three Roman gods who have something to do with agriculture and rural life; Bacchus, in particular, being the god of wine; and therefore all stand to some extent for the enjoyment of food and drink. James may simply be running on, babbling of the three in a foolish, disconnected way: it would seem so.

TAP = Cask or (more probably) vintage - a good year for wine.

MACHIAVEL = The crafty schemer (from Nicolo Machiavelli, of Florence, who died in 1525; noted for his cunning diplomacy`.

´NUNC VINO PELLITE CURAS, CRAS INGENS ITERABIMUS AEQUOR´ = ´Drive away your cares with wine now: tomorrow we shall embark upon the mighty ocean´ (Horace´s Odes, I, 7).

BACCHANALIAN = Follower of the god of wine.

MAUDLIN = Shedding tears of drunkenness (a reference to paintings which portrayed Mary Magdalene weeping).

POT-HOUSE = Ale-house; tavern.

ATROCIOUS = Cruel [Latin Ātrox].

FACETIOUS = Humorous [Latin Facētus, ´witty´ or ´merry´; probably more merry than witty - as we should say, ´trying to be funny´, but not really succeeding].

PUGILISTIC = Having to do with boxing, or fist-fighting [Latin Pugnus, ´fist´].

JOCULAR = Joking [Latin Joculus, ´a little joke´].

TIPSY = Drunken [Provincial German Tipps, ´drunkenness´].

THOROUGH DRAUGHT = a through draught; wind blowing through the window into the house.

MENACED = Threatened. We use ´menaced´ of people who are threatened: it is interesting to see Thackeray using it of someone who does the threatening.

PELISSE = Here, evidently a three-quarter length cloak with cape or hood, and slits for the wearer´s arms [Latin Pellis, ´skin´; from which we get ´pelt´]. The word comes via Italian, and John Florio (born in London in 1553 of Italian parents; published more than one dictionary) defines Peliccia as ´any kind of furred garment´; but it ultimately came to mean different things at different times, and could refer to silk garments, children´s garments, and so on, according to the fashion. Lady Mary Wortley-Montagu´s Letters (1718) possibly describe what Becky had made pretty well exactly, in her phrase, ´a pellice of rich brocade lined with sables´.

NICKNACKS = Trinkets; trifles [also spelt Nick-knacks and Knick-knacks].

JOCKEYED = Cheated.

SPIRITUELLE = Witty, lively, shrewd, intelligent - all the things which Miss Crawley would like to think are true of her.

RAFFOLES OF = Dotes on; raves about.

ESPIEGLE = Roguish; mischievous.

TOQUE = Bonnet; head-dress [Armoric (the language of the Celtic inhabitants of Brittany, the north-western part of France, who lived Ar, 'on' or 'beside' Mor, 'the sea') Tok]; though the word could mean 'a sort of triangular cushion of horsehair...fastened on the female head', over which 'the hair was erected, and crisped and frizzed' (Maria Edgeworth's apology for the Jews, entitled Harrington, 1817).

PROTEGEE = Young woman under the care and protection of an older and more distinguished person.

ENTREE = Free access; an opening; by way of being accepted.

CORDONS = Ribbons, in a rather special sense, as of an Order of honour (such as, in our day, The Most Excellent Order of the British Empire).

DUNS = Creditors (or their agents) pressing for payment of debts.

CONTRETEMPS = Untoward event; unfortunate happening.

FÊTES = Festivities; merrymakings.

GALIGNANI'S JOURNAL = In fact, Galignani's Messenger, founded by Giovanni Antonio Galignani in 1814 in Paris, was substantially improved by his sons John Anthony and William when he died in 1821. It was widely read by English residents and visitors in Europe, because it advocated friendship between France and England.

HYMENEAL = In effect, honeymoon (Greek Humen, god of marriage).

CHAPTER 35

INTELLIGENCE = News.

CATALOGUE = ´Thorough reckoning´ [Greek].

NO CONFIDANT = No one to confide in; no one to think aloud to.

´PAX IN BELLO´ = ´Peace in war´

SUPERSCRIPTION = Address on the envelope (by which is meant the name of the person intended to receive the letter; not necessarily where he lived).

BALKED = Thwarted [Old English <u>Balca</u>, ´ridge´; at first, ´a strip of land left unploughed´; then ´a beam of wood´; finally, a barrier or hindrance].

<u>DULCE ET DECORUM EST PRO PATRIA MORI</u> = It is pleasant and honourable to die for one´s country (which is what most people feel till a relative of theirs is killed).

DECLIVITY = Slope downwards [Latin <u>De</u>-, ´down´ + <u>Clīvus</u>, ´slope´].

CUIRASSES = Breastplates, originally of leather [Latin <u>Coriacea</u>, ´of leather´. To excoriate is to skin something, and to score was originally to make a cut in a piece of skin].

LACKEY = Man-servant [French <u>Laquais</u>, ´footman´].

STRAITENED = Poverty-stricken [Anglo-French <u>Estreit</u>; ultimately from Latin <u>Strictus</u>, ´drawn tightly´ - as of purse-strings which one cannot afford to unloose].

IMPRECATIONS = Prayers that calamity may befall someone. Mr Osborne is going on about George´s disobedience in marrying Amelia [Latin <u>In</u>-, ´against´ + <u>Precāri</u>, ´to pray´].

PITTANCE = Small allowance [French <u>Pittance</u>, which originally meant a gift made out of pity].

CATASTROPHE = Disaster [Greek, ´over-turning´].

HAPLESS = Unlucky [Icelandic <u>Happ</u>, ´good fortune´ + less, ´without´].

PAPBOATS = Boat-shaped containers of semi-liquid food for babies.

CORALS = Toys or playthings made of smoothly polishly coral, which it would be safe for a baby who was teething to put into his mouth and bite on.

DANDLE = Pet; fondle; move lightly up and down [Italian <u>Dandola</u>, ´a doll´; hence, to dandle is to treat as a little girl would treat a doll].

PERSPICUITY = Ease of understanding [Latin <u>Per-</u>, ´through; thoroughly; completely; + <u>Specere</u>, ´to look´].

CHAPTER 36

EQUIPAGE = Carriage with horses, harness, and so on [Old Norse <u>Skipa</u>, ´(to fit out and man) a sailing-ship´].

JOBBED = Hired.

BOARD-WAGES = Wages which kept servants in food and drink while the family was away, and there were few duties or appearance to keep up.

HOB-AND-NOBBING = Literally, ´have and not have´; that is, ´Drink, or not, as you please´: hence, to be on intimate terms with people [Anglo-Saxon <u>Habban ne habban</u>´].

PARVENUE = Upstart; newcomer [Latin <u>Pervenīre</u>, ´to arrive´].

<u>RÉUNIONS</u> = Parties; get-togethers: receptions.

<u>FRACAS</u> = Disturbance; quarrel.

BLACK-LEG = One who wins at billiards or cards by cheating.

DALLIANCE = Time spent in aimless pleasure.

TRIFLING = Indulgence in light amusements; wasting time for fun.

<u>TOUPÉE</u> = Small wig [diminutive (´small version´) of <u>Toupe</u>, ´tuft´].

DILIGENCE = Short for <u>Carosse de diligence</u>, or fast coach.

<u>PREMIER</u> = First floor, which had the biggest and best appointed rooms.

<u>ENTRESOL</u> = Low-ceilinged floor between the first floor and the ground floor.

<u>BONNE</u> = Servant-girl.

<u>SERRED</u> = Locked up; locked away.

PELISSE = In this instance, a sleeveless garment worn over a dress when walking out; possibly what we should now call a pelisse-robe or day-dress fastened all down the front with ribbon-bows or concealed hooks and eyes.

<u>CETTE CHARMANTE</u> = That attractive.

<u>DE RETOUR</u> = Coming back.

<u>AVEC SA FEMME</u> – <u>UNE PETITE DAME</u>, <u>TRÈS SPIRITUELLE</u> = With his lady; a little lady, very sprightly.

<u>AH MONSIEUR!</u> <u>ILS M´ONT AFFREUSEMENT VOLÉ</u> = Ah Sir! They robbed me frightfully.

<u>ACCRUING TO</u> = To be gained from (strictly, amassing to his credit, as in a bank account) [Anglo-French <u>Acrewe</u>, ´growth´].

<u>BREAD-CAKE</u> = Bread of the quality of cake.

<u>MILITAIRE</u> = Soldier.

CHAPTER 37

MONTÉES = Furnished.

PERQUISITES = Rewards over and above the wages agreed [Latin Perquisitum, 'something sought out'].

CLANDESTINELY = Secretly [Latin Clam].

VENDING = Selling; offering for sale [Latin Venum, 'sale'].

HAMMER = The auctioneer, who uses one to signal that a sale has been agreed.

PRODIGIOUS = Marvellous [Latin Prōdigiōsus].

CHEVAL GLASS = A hinged looking-glass, mounted on a frame, and big enough to reflect the whole figure [French A cheval, 'as on horseback'; mounted, with one foot - or, in this case, hinge - on each side].

SILHOUETTE = Portrait in outline, filled in with black [Étienne de Silhouette, French minister of finance in 1759, was thus mocked for his petty economies].

FLAGS = Standards hanging from ceremonial trumpets.

PERIWIGS = Small wigs [French Perruque].

DÉJEUNER = Lunch (the picture is of a small marquee, and a buffet in the garden).

PURVEYORS = Caterers [Anglo-French Purveier, 'to provide'. The word provisions means food and drink].

PERTINACITY = Persistence [Latin for 'holding on tightly' - Pertinax].

SERVANTS' PORTER = Abbreviation for porters' beer (that is, a type of beer popular among porters), which was dark brown and bitter, made from malt which was partly charred as a result of being dried at high temperature.

FLIPPANCY = Fluent, confident speech; nimbleness (from flip, 'to move with a jerk'): not, as it means now, 'displaying unbecoming levity, or humour'.

DEMURE = Affectedly solemn or stately [French De moeurs, ´mannerly´].

DANDIES = Men dressed in special finery - clothes so smart as to be showy, or ostentatious.

METROPOLIS = Mother-city (that is, the mother of cities) [Greek].

GENTEEL = Elegantly fashionable [from the French Gentil, ´noble; aristocratic´; but always in a playful or sarcastic sense - not really noble; not really aristocratic: trying to be so].

CALLING OUT = Challenging to a duel.

DOMESTICS = Household servants [Latin Domus, ´home´].

BROUGHAM = One-horse closed carriage, with two or four wheels, for two or four people [after the first Lord Brougham & Vaux].

BONS VIVANTS = ´Gay dogs´; lovers of pleasure; epicures.

HUCKSTER´S STALL = Market-stall of a street-trader [the name refers to the trader´s back, bent in carrying a pack; for the original hucksters were hawkers, or door-to-door salesman: akin to the German Höcken, ´to take on one´s back´].

CAMEL-LEOPARD = Giraffe [Latin Camelus, ´a camel´ + Pardalis, ´a leopard´].

I PROPOSE = I bid; I declare [that is, am about to show] my card.

I MARK THE KING = I put the king [as it might be, of hearts] on the table, to score.

I MARK THE TRICK = I complete the round - I play the last card due to be played.

SCONCES = Candlesticks on wall-brackets [Old French Esconse, ´lantern´].

BUCK-TEETH = Protruding, like the teeth of a rabbit.

CORYDON = A shepherd in the Idylls of Theocritus and the Eclogues of Virgil, whose name is conventional in pastoral poetry.

MELIBAEUS = One of the interlocutors (people conversing) in the first Eclogue of Virgil (70-19 BC), whose Eclogues imitated the pastoral poems of Theocritus (310-250 BC); both, poets of ancient Greece.

FREDAINES = Wild oats; pranks; misdeeds.

MOLLIFIED = Pacified; appeased [Latin Mollificāre, ´to soften´].

WITHOUT THE CIRCLE = Outside the circle.

GARRET = Attic [French Guérite, ´sentry-box; cabin´].

BONNE = Servant-girl.

SWEETMEATS = Confectionery; what we now call ´sweeties´.

GAMBOLS = Capers; leaps [Italian Gamba, ´leg´; hence, a vigorous movement of the leg].

VIVIFIED FIGURE = Tailor's dummy brought to life.

MAGASIN DES MODES = Fashion-designer's place of business; couturier's.

HOLLAND = Linen-fabric originally made in Holland.

MAITRE D'HÔTEL = Head waiter; butler.

REPINING = Complaining [Latin Re-, 'intense' + Poenam 'pain'].

CHAPTER 38

FURLOUGH = Leave of absence [Dutch Verlof].

INCURRED = Caused; cost [Latin Incurrere, 'to run into; to bring upon oneself'].

COMMISSION LOTTERY-AGENT = An agent for raffle-tickets.

AGIOS = Premiums on money 'in exchange' - that is, a percentage charged for cashing bank-notes [Italian Aggio, 'premium; excess charge over the nominal value']. Agios are sometimes required today by English shopkeepers on Scottish bank-notes: the Scot tenders a pound-note, and gets, say, 95p in return.

PATRONISE YOU = Treat you in a condescending way [Latin Patronus, 'protector'; from Pater, 'father'].

ZANIES = Clowns [Italian Giovanni, the name 'John' used derisively, as a target for mirth].

KNAVES = Rascals [Old English Cnafa, 'boy'].

MUNOZ = Augustin Munoz (pronounced 'Moon-yoth') was Duke of Rinsares from about 1810 till 1873, and morganatic husband of Maria Christina, Queen of Spain. The story is as follows: in 1829, King Ferdinand VII of Spain married his niece, Maria Christina of Naples. In 1830, their daughter (who became Isabella II when she was declared of age to rule, in 1843) was born. In 1833, Ferdinand died, and Maria Christina was declared Regent (or ruler till her daughter was old enough to rule). About 1836, Maria Christina married Augustin Munoz (whom Chambers's Encyclopedia describes as 'a guardsman') - secretly, to preserve her regency. In 1837, Maria Christina went into exile, returning as Queen Mother in 1845. In 1868, Isabella fled to France, and Spain was in effect (what we call de facto) a republic, becoming a republic officially (de jure) in 1873. The monarchy was restored in 1875, when Alfonso XII: the son of Don Carlos (Don Carlos having been promised the throne by some people in 1812): came to the throne.

When Vanity Fair was published, in 1847, poor Munoz would have appeared particularly useless.

HUNTERS = Horses used in hunting, and therefore particularly fine animals.

RANCOROUS = Bitter-tongued; spiteful [Latin <u>Rancidus</u>, ´loathsome´].

HARRIDANS = Ugly old women [French <u>Haridelle</u>, ´a worn-out horse´]. Notice that, as often when writers try to improve a meaningful noun, Thackeray does not need his second adjective: it would have said as much to call them rancorous harridans.

PARLIAMENT = Short for parliament-cake; a thin, crisp, rectangular ginger-bread cake (c 1812).

DAFFY´S ELIXIR = A tranquilliser popular for 200 years. It got a bad reputation when people began lacing it - mixing it - with gin. It was this lacing with gin that Amelia remembers (unjustly, in connection with her mother) when she talks of ´poison´.

CROUP = Inflammation of the wind-pipe (tracheitis, if you want the learned word for it) characterized by a peculiarly sharp, ringing cough.

MOPE = To be dull and listless [akin to Swedish <u>Mopa</u>, ´to sulk´].

A VIPER IN YOUR BOSOM = The bosom does not in fact mean the breast: it means the crook of one´s arm. The meaning was transferred in popular fancy because the crook of the arm was where a baby was held by its mother to be nourished at the breast. The populace would think of one thing while speaking of the other (as it does in other ways which will occur to the reader).

DEJEUNERS = Luncheons [Latin <u>Disjējūnāre</u>, ´to break one´s fast´].

TAMARINDS = Pods whose pith was medicinal [Arabic <u>Tamr-Hind</u>, ´the date of India´].

CHEVALIER = A chivalrous man; either a very courteous man or an actual member of the lowest order of French nobility.

PERFIDIOUS ALBION = Faithless Britain (a Continental expression used when Europeans wished to refer to the United Kingdom in a critical or contemptuous way; not unlike the ´damn Yankees´ we call Americans when we are displeased with the United States) [<u>Albion</u> is a reference to the white cliffs of Dover].

REINE DES AMOURS = Queen of the [mythological] Loves.

LACKADAISICAL CREATURE = As though she were for ever moaning, ´Lack a day! oh, lack a day´.

CRIBBAGE = A game of cards in which the dealer receives a crib (or extra hand) drawn partly from the hands of his opponents (a ´hand´ being an allotment of cards per person).

---<u>s</u>. PER CHALDRON = So many shillings per dry measure, varying from 32 to 36 bushels or more, according to the locality [=Cauldron, from the Latin <u>Caldus</u>, ´hot´].

CANVASSED = Applied for orders [Greek <u>Cannabis</u>, ´hemp´. The verb, ´to canvass´, meant to strain or sieve - sieves being made at first of the coarse, hempen cloth called canvas].

OUTCRY = Auction (from the shouting-out of bids by the auctioneer).

JACK KETCH = Public executioner from 1663.

CONTUMELIOUSLY = Rudely and contemptuously [Latin <u>Contumēlia</u>, ´an insult´].

A BOX OF WHICH PLACE OF ENTERTAINMENT = A small room.

LISPED OUT = Hissed [Anglo-Saxon <u>Wlisp</u>].

DOMINEERING = Ruling over; ordering about [Dutch <u>Domineren</u>, ´to rule´].

CHAPTER 39

SYCOPHANTIC = Flattering [inexplicably from the Greek <u>Phanein</u>, ´to show´ + <u>Sukos</u>, ´a fig´].

HYPOCRITICAL = Insincere [Greek <u>Hupokrites</u>, ´an actor´]. The true word is <u>Hypocrital</u>, for the noun is <u>Hypocrite</u>; otherwise it would be <u>Hypocritic</u>. Language has many instances of a word changing its form to match another which most users know better.

RETRENCH = Reduce expenses; economise; cut down on ´spending [Old French <u>Retrencher</u>, ´to cut back´].

MILLINERS´ FURNITURE = Items furnished by milliners - hats, gloves, scarves, &c [all originally made best at Milan, and sold by Milaners].

COUNTY BULBUL = Egyptian nightingale - <u>the</u> nightingale of the County.

INVEIGLE = Entice [Latin <u>Ab-</u>, ´without´ + <u>Oculi</u>, ´eyes´; hence, to seek to lead someone as though he were blind].

MALMSEY = A strong sweet wine from Monemvasia in Greece (36.5^{O}N, 23°E), or from the island of Madeira, 400 miles west of Morocco; 33°N, 17°W.

BOOBY = Fool [Spanish <u>Bobo</u>].

BACKGAMMON = Game for two, with draughtsmen, board and dice [´Back-game´; pieces taken being put back on the board].

SALVER = Tray [Latin <u>Salvus</u>, ´safe´: from the Spanish <u>Salva</u> - the tray on which a cup was placed after being tasted for poison].

BOXED = Hit; cuffed [Middle English].

CHATTELS = Property other than freehold [Latin <u>Capitālis</u>, ´capital´].

BOOZED = Guzzled liquor [Dutch <u>Buizen</u>, ´to drink heavily; to gulp´].

SCREWED HIS TENANTS = Pressed his tenants for money (like Mr <u>Screwge</u> in Dickens´s <u>A Christmas Carol</u>).

DOTAGE = Imbecility caused by old age; what the physicians call senile dementia [akin to Old Norse <u>Dotta</u>, ´to nod from sleep´].

RIGOUR = Inflexibility [Latin <u>Rigor</u>, ´stiffness; harshness; rudeness; numbness; cold´ - what a lot the Latin synonyms tell us about the word!].

CALASH = Originally, a light, two-horse carriage [Greek <u>Kalesche</u>, ´something with wheels´]. Here, a bonnet which folds back like the top of a calash, and therefore ordinarily projects beyond the face.

PRESSES AND ESCRITOIRES = (1) Presses were up-right cupboards in which clothes and other things were kept. (2) Escritoires were writing desks with lockable lids and drawers [the French word is now <u>Ecritoire</u>, from Latin <u>Scriptōrium</u>, from <u>Scrībere</u>, ´to write´].

AN EXPRESS WAS SENT OFF = A messenger.

CHAPTER 40

MULTIFARIOUS = Made up of many different items [Late Latin, ´manifold´].

CALOMEL = A white, tasteless powder of mercurous chloride, used as a purgative or laxative [Greek <u>Kalos melas</u>, ´beautiful black´ - the powder was black before, at a certain point in its preparation, it turned white].

ASSIDUITY = Application; sticking to one´s duties [Latin <u>Assiduus</u>, ´sitting close´].

GRUEL = Broth, usually made with oatmeal [Old French, from mediaeval Latin <u>Grutellum</u>, the diminutive - indicating a little only - of <u>Grūtum</u>, ´meal´].

INCUMBRANCES = The old form of Encumbrances = liabilities, such as a mortgage, feu duty, &c [Old French <u>Encombrance</u>, ´obstacle; obstruction; burden´].

VACILLATION = Wavering [Latin, <u>Vacillāre</u>, ´to sway to and fro´].

DEPOSE = Put down; ´take down a peg´ [Latin <u>Depōnere</u>, ´to pull down´]. Strictly, Thackeray is thinking of Lady Southdown as the ruler of the family; and a ruler who is forced to give up the throne in favour of another monarch is said to have been deposed.

MISSIVE = Short for Letter Missive; that is, a letter from a superior, conveying a command [Mediaeval Latin <u>Missīvus</u>, ´sent´].

TRAVEL BODKIN = To sit wedged between two where there is room for two only.

FROCK = Gown opening at the back, worn by women and children [Latin <u>Floccosa</u>, ´made of wool´]; in this case, a mourning-garment.

SILENUS = The satyr who attended Bacchus, the Roman god of wine.

DISSENTING SHOEMAKER´S LADY = The wife of a shoemaker who attended a nonconformist chapel (probably what was called a Congregational church, because its doctrines were decided by the congregation).

MOREEN = Watered wool (that is, wool having a wavy appearance on its surface), or wool and cotton; a heavy fabric made in imitation of mohair [Arabic <u>Mokhayyar</u>, meaning cloth made of the hair of the Angora goat; the cloth being silky, and the goat coming originally from Ankara, the capital of Turkey: 40°N, 33°E.

RENCONTRE = Meeting [French <u>Rencontre</u>, ´re-encounter´]; in particular, a meeting by chance.

CHAPTER 41

INSINUATING = Winding into [Latin <u>Sinuāre</u>, ´to wind´ + <u>In-</u>, ´into´]; the Cambridge lad was described toward the end of chapter 7; and he wound Rebecca up (or, to use Thackeray´s words from chapter 7, <u>covered</u> her up) in one of his Benjamins, or coats. Thackeray here is using a word which can mean ´to hint´; but chapter 7 conveys no impression of the Cambridge lad hinting at anything: so the word cannot be a pun here.

CRAPE = Thin material, such as silk or cotton, with a ridged surface [French <u>Crepe</u>, from Latin <u>Crispus</u>, ´curled´].

BUGLES = Tubular glass beads, usually black. The word Bugle is short for Bugle-horn; which shows us where the idea of the tube comes from: but Bugle itself comes from the Latin <u>Buculus</u>, ´young ox´; showing us where the actual horn originated.

HABITED IN SABLE = Dressed in black fur [Old French <u>Habit</u>, ´clothing´; Icelandic <u>Safal</u>, ´a small, four-legged animal].

SCUTCHEON = Interesting as an example of aphesis (the process by which a word loses its first letter unintentionally: you will find many more, from [e]squire to [ap]ply-wood). The original here was escutcheon [Latin <u>Scutum</u>, ´shield´], meaning the shield on which a coat of arms is painted. Thackeray, of course, is being funny when he imagines a coat of arms depicting a coal-scuttle.

WATCHERS = It was customary for vigil - wakefulness - to be kept by the coffin in Thackeray´s lifetime; partly out of respect for the deceased - and partly against the incursion [´the running in (and out)´] of thieves. Such watchers were often temporary employees, as many ´mourners´ were till recent times. When you think of it, the undertaker´s men are professional mourners now.

REGENCY = Rule during the Sovereign´s absence or indisposition (Thackeray is being playful here) - it can also mean ´the division of a country into regions´; knowledge of which fact would have spared us the solecism [´wrong word´] Regionalization.

BLACK DOSE = Probably an infusion [´soaking in water, to extract the soluble properties´]) of senna pods - from the Pudding Pipe tree (or <u>Cassia fistula</u>) of

India; containing a pulp used as a laxative - with sulphate of magnesia, known as black draught. Ugh!

CALUMNIATED = Spoke evil of, falsely [Latin Calumniāri, 'to blame falsely'].

RENDEZVOUS = Meeting place [French, 'Meet you ....'].

POINTER = A dog trained to face where a shot bird has fallen to earth.

IMBECILITY = Weakness of mind or body; here, weak-mindness [Latin Imbēcillitās, 'weakness'; literally, 'without a staff (to lean on)'].

SUBSISTED = Existed; continued to be [Latin Sub-, 'Up' + Sistere, 'to stand']. The word has delicate shades of meaning, because Sub- indicates a change of position; in this case, from a lower to a higher; and Subsist means basically, 'to support life': so that, in this single word, Thackeray is giving us a picture of a relationship which hardly mattered to old Sir Pitt while he was hale and hearty, but which withstood the changes of his health and fortune which deprived him of almost every other consolation, and gave him something to live for - slight as it might be, something to hang on to, in his heart - as death approached.

MORTIFICATION = Sharp regret; chagrin [Latin Mors, 'death' + Facere, 'to make' - 'I'd thought I'd die' (with embarrassment)].

PALLS = Cloths to spread over a coffin [Latin Pallium, 'a cloak'].

DRAGOON = Cavalryman of a regiment armed with muskets 'breathing fire' [like a dragon]; alternatively, armed with pistols whose hammers where a particular shape. The former is more likely, because the first dragoons were raised by Marshal Brissac in 1660, and their short carbines - short, for use on horseback - had the representation of a dragon's head at the muzzle. Similar regiments were formed in the British Army, whose equipment divided them into Light or Heavy Dragoons.

PONY-CHAISE = Light, open carriage [French Chaire; which became Chaise by a peculiarity of Parisian speech in the fifteenth and sixteenth centuries] with a low dashboard and often a single seat, suspended by leather above an ornate wooden frame: introduced c 1760.

PALINGS = Stakes used in fencing, fixed upright in the ground, or joined top and bottom with a rail [Latin Pālus, 'post', as in 'gate-post']. When we talk of something being 'beyond the pale', we mean the territory enclosed by such fencing - and we talk of it usually in a metaphorical sense, meaning that it would be done by some people, but not by our set; our group, &c.

WORSTED = Fine, soft woollen yarn for knitting (from the town of Worstead, in Norfolk, where it was first made: on the A149, thirteen miles SE by S of Cromer).

DUNS = People pressing for payment.

SCREWS OF TOBACCO = Twists; pipefuls.

THE BRAND WHO 'HONOURED' THE LETTER = The bearer, who was otherwise sure to go to hell after her death.

LOTH = Reluctant [Old English Láth, 'hostile; hateful'].

CHAPTER 42

DIRE = Dismal; terrible [Latin Dīrus, ´ominous; unfortunate; terrible´].

HUMDRUM = Monotonous; dull [to hum is to make a low, continuous sound like a bee. The verb was turned into an adjective by adding a rhyming monosyllable to the verb, so that it resembled what it stood for, more than ever].

PLATE = Plates, dishes and cutlery (originally all of silver and gold; eventually, often covered with a thin sheet of silver or gold, and therefore still worth much) [ultimately from Latin Plānus, ´flat; which developed in two surprising ways: in one, the L shrank and became an I, becoming the musician´s Piano; in the other, by mediaeval times, the word became Plattus, ´flat´, and so, Plate].

APPURTENANCES = Accessories; the things which belong to - here, an heiress [French Appartenance, ´thing owned by someone´].

WOFUL = Old spelling of Woeful; sad [Old English Wéa, ´grief´ + Full: ´Full of grief´].

RUPTURE = Breach of friendly relations; not being on speaking terms with those one knew well [Late Latin Ruptūra, ´a breaking´].

NOB = Superficially, this would be the sort of abbreviation written against a man´s name to distinguish a Nob[leman] from a Gent[leman], as it might be, in a parish register; but some dictionaries say that it comes from the Scottish word Knabb, ´a person of consequence´.

MESALLIANCE = A discreditable marriage, because with someone socially beneath him.

ONTRYS = Entrées [French for dishes of meat served between other courses: Entre means ´between´].

SWARREYS = Soirées [French word meaning ´evening parties´].

AUGURED = Foretold; prophesied [Latin Augur, ´one who foretold the future from the behaviour of birds´].

CONSOLE GLASS = Mirror fixed by brackets to the wall [French; possibly from Consolider, ´to make firm; to strengthen´].

BROWN HOLLAND BAG = Bag made of cotton which has been treated to make it opaque and rather stiff [such bags originally came from Holland].

CORDOVAN LEATHER = Soft, smooth, leather originally made of goatskin, at Cordova in southern Spain: now known as Cordoba; $38^{\circ}N$, $5^{\circ}W$.

SERJEANT = A barrister of a distinctly superior kind which no longer exists by that name, not unlike the Queen's Counsel of today.

A HANGING JUDGE = The sort of judge who always passed the severest sentence available to him.

TAWNY PORT = An after-dinner wine of better quality than ruby port, but not as good as vintage port (Andre Simon says that vintage port is the only port worth drinking).

DISSOLUTE = Loose-living; late-to-bed-and-late-to-rise; reckless in the pursuit of pleasure [Latin Dissolūtus, 'negligent'].

NAMBY-PAMBY = Weakly sentimental (after the poetry off Ambrose Philips, 1675?-1749, of St. John's College, Cambridge - making fun of his first name. Such word-play can work the other way round: Sir James Barrie was fond of Margaret, the little daughter of the poet, W E Henley. Her pet-name for Barrie was 'Friendy'; which eventually became 'Friendy-wendy'. The word 'Wendy' stuck in his mind, and he used this accidentally made-up nonsense-word as the name for the heroine of Peter Pan].

SCOUTED IT = Treated it with contempt; rejected it with scorn [Icelandic Skuta, 'taunt'].

CHAPTER 43

TIFFIN = Light mid-day meal [from slang <u>Tiff</u>, ´to drink or sip´].

HOOKAH = A water-casket through which tobacco-smoke is drawn, to cool it [Urdu <u>Huqqah</u>].

CANTONMENT = Military quarters or lodgings [Italian <u>Cantone</u>, ´corner´ - as of a barrack-square + <u>-ment</u>, a suffix indicating the result of action - the soldier has been ´cornered´, or ´quartered´, or billeted in those lodgings].

ZENANAS = East Indian harems (the women´s quarters in a Mohammedan family) [Hindi <u>Zanana</u>, from Persian <u>Zan</u>, ´woman´].

PUISNE JUDGE = Literally, junior judge; judge presiding over a lower court [surprisingly, Puny is the same word; from the Latin <u>Post</u>, ´after´ + <u>Ne</u>, ´born´ - hence, ´younger´, and therefore ´less strong´].

<u>LASSATA NONDUM SATIATA RECESSIT</u> = ´Wearied but still not satisfied, she withdrew´: a daring reference to Messalina, the promiscuous wife of the Roman emperor, Tiberius Claudius Nero Germanicus (10 BC - 54 AD), who, Juvenal (in Satire VI) tells us, ´rose up weary but unsatisfied´.

CABAL = Intrigue; a plan by a group of people to promote their ideas by secret agreement [the word is an acronym composed of the initials of King Charles II´s ministers, Clifford, Ashley, Buckingham, Arlington and Lauderdale, who did just that].

DELIRIUM TREMENS = A state of wild fantasy which results from drinking too much for days on end [Latin <u>Delirare</u>, ´to drive the furrow awry´ in ploughing: <u>De-</u>, ´from´ + <u>Lira</u>, ´the furrow´: hence, to rave; to be crazy].

SUBJUGATE = Overcome; conquer [Latin <u>Subjugare</u>, ´to put under the yoke´, from <u>Sub-</u>, meaning ´change to a lower position´ + <u>Jugum</u>, ´yoke´ - as of oxen].

DEPOTS = Headquarters of regiments [Latin <u>Depositum</u>, ´thing stored´].

PALANKIN = Now spelt Palanquin, meaning ´a covered litter´, or bed on which people of distinction were carried about [East Indian <u>Palanki</u>, becoming Portuguese

83

Palanquim; both deriving from the Pali (language used in Buddhist sacred writings) word, Pâlangki].

SNIPES = Birds living in marshy places. They have long bills, and most European names for them resemble the word Snipe, which has given us Sniper ('a marksman'; now, aiming for a human target).

CHEROOTS = Small, thin cigars [Tamil Shuruttu, 'a roll of tobacco-leaf' - the word Cigar itself means a roll of tobacco-leaves].

SIMPERING = Smiling in a silly, affected way [Danish Simper, 'coy'].

GRIZZLED = Turned grey [French Grisel, from Gris, 'grey'].

JET RINGLETS = Hair in ringlets, in colour like the glossy, deep-black coal of Gagai (c 30°N, 37°E), in Lycia, Asia Minor - coal so compact, and susceptible of such a polish, that it was wrought into buttons and ornaments [the Greek name for Gagai was Gagates, which in French became successively Gayet, Jayet and Jeat].

KILLING PINK FROCK = Sure to make everyone fall in love with her ('Madam! You slay me with your beauty', an affected young man might say).

HEARTLESS = Disheartened; dejected [Heartless is one of a number of words whose meaning has not so much changed as focused on a shade of meaning which was always there, in such a way as to imply that it could not mean anything else. One was heartless if one had no heart for a job: 'My heart isn't in it'. It is now used in conversation as thought it must mean 'cruel' - 'Have you no heart?' Other words whose original meaning tends to be overlooked or denied are, Presently ['now'], Grateful ['giving cause of gratitude'] and Hopeful ['giving cause for hope'; so that Hopefully does indeed basically mean 'I hope that it is or will be so'].

PERUSAL = Careful reading [Latin Per-, 'thoroughly' + Ūsus, 'experience'].

NEGLIGENCE = Neglect [Latin Neg-, 'not' + Legere, 'to pick up'].

NUPTIAL CHAMBER = What we should now call the honeymoon suite [Latin Nūbere, 'to marry' + Chamber - 'room'].

PAPILLOTES = Curl-papers [French Papillon, 'butterfly' (which a curl-paper looks rather like].

PARLEY = Talk; discuss [French Parler, 'to speak' - giving us Parliament, where people do].

CHAPTER 44

SALMI = A ragoût (or stew) of partly roasted game (pheasants, partridges, hare, &c) stewed with wine, bread and condiments (seasonings; spices); a relish (or savoury) [perhaps an abbreviation of Salmagundi (French <u>Salmigondis</u>), meaning a dish of chopped meat, eggs, anchovies and pickled cabbage; the traditional Salmi was a ragoût of woodcock, larks and thrushes]. The third paragraph down tells us that Becky's salmi, in this instance, was made with pheasants and white wine from Tain; a little town twelve miles north of Valence beside the river Rhône: 45°N, 5°E.

CUDDLED = Not necessarily what we should mean by the word, but coddled him; made much of him; pampered [Latin <u>Cadel</u>, 'an animal born prematurely', and therefore weak, and in need of special care].

HARANGUES = Pompous speeches [ultimately from Old High German <u>Hrinc</u>, 'a ring or circle'; hence Italian <u>Aringa</u>, 'speech made to a ring of people', and the French word <u>Harangue</u> (ditto). The old German word gave us our skating rink].

MAIL = Mail coach [Gaelic <u>Mala</u>, 'bag', in which letters were carried].

MUM = Not given to speaking [in imitation of the murmur, "M'm", which is all such people usually say].

STRAITENED = Restricted; hemmed in; limited; pressed by poverty [Old French <u>Estreit</u>, 'narrow', from Latin <u>Strictus</u>, 'drawn tight']. The notion ultimately comes from the origin of our word String, the thin cord with which would be drawn tight the neck of a money bag - and drawing cord tightly round the neck turns the word String into Strangle: both come from the Latin <u>Stringere</u>, 'to draw tight'.

INCUMBRANCES = Legal claims on the estate [Latin <u>Incombrāre</u>, from <u>In</u>-, 'against' + <u>Combrus</u>, 'an obstacle']. We now spell the word as Encumbrances.

PANTALOONS = Pair of trousers [originally, breeches and stockings worn as one garment, like the 'tights' of women today, and the garment of a stock character in old Italian comedy, called Pantalone; after San Pantaleone ('the All-merciful') of Venice. He was martyred in AD 305, and revered in the Middle Ages as a patron saint of physicians second only to St. Luke].

LANDING-PLACE = What we call the landing; a resting-place after the first (or only) flight of stairs.

DISCOVERED = Uncovered; revealed; disclosed [a shade of meaning which Discovered has always had].

INQUISITION = Nothing like the Spanish Inquisition ['court for the examination and punishment of heretics'], but merely an investigation (with shades of the old meanings, Stare or Scrutiny - 'a looking-into' - combined with the idea of Inquisitiveness, 'troublesomely curious and ready to pry').

CALUMNY = Slander [Latin Calumnia, 'false accusation']. Thackeray is using the word as though it were the name of a person, because (he is saying in effect) there is always a servant ready to say false things about people behind their backs.

JANISSARY = One of the guard of the Sultan of Turkey (a sultan is the ruler of any Mohammedan country; but the Sultan of Turkey was known as 'the Sultan of Sultans') who, for security reasons, recruited his guard from the fourteenth to the nineteenth centuries from the children of his Christian subjects [Turkish Yeni, 'new' + Tcheri, 'soldiers']. The Christian subjects, it should be added, were all slaves.

VEHMGERICHT = Royal tribunal which maintained public order from the twelfth to the fourteenth centuries in Westphalia (52°N, 7°E: the southern part of Saxony; some 180 miles southwest of the coast of Holland), and which had jurisdiction over people of high rank as well as low.

ARTIFICER = Constructor; maker (here, weaver) [Latin Artifex, 'craftsman'].

COMFORTERS = Knitted woollen scarves.

FLAGS = Flag-stones which paved the floor (what we call flags are pieces of cloth in the shape of such stones) [Icelandic Flaga, 'a slab of stone'].

BAND AND BONNET BOXES = Boxes made of pasteboard (cardboard made by pasting single sheets of paper together, or of papiermache) or of thin, flexible pieces of wood and paper, for holding articles of clothing.

CHAPTER 45

TO DRAW HIS COUNTRY = To have the huntsman force the fox to break cover and run for its life, on Sir Pitt's land.

CHAPTERS = Councils comprising the clergymen attached to cathedrals, presided over by Deans; so the Dean was chairman of the Chapter [Old French <u>Chapitre</u>, from Latin <u>Capitulum</u>, 'a little head'. The idea is, that, under the appropriate heading for the day, a short lesson from the Bible was read in some services of the Latin Church: such a lesson was called a chapter; indeed, the Bible was divided into chapters for this very purpose; but the <u>name</u> Chapter was gradually transferred, first, to the meeting at which the lesson was read, and finally to the people who met to hear it].

THE TWO WHIPS = Short for Whippers-in, who kept the hounds from wandering off, and whipped them into the pack when necessary.

RAW-BONED = Here, lean and large-boned.

RATING = Chiding, scolding or vehemently reproving; ticking off [Middle English; usually expanded into Berating].

SPATTERDASHED = In leggings [usually abbreviated to Spats]; garments to prevent mud bespattering the wearer.

HACKS = Horses used for ordinary work.

HUNTERS = Horses kept for hunting because of their special qualities.

BICKERINGS = Fightings [Welsh <u>Bicra</u>].

CORTEGE = Procession (not necessarily a funeral procession, but any procession if sufficiently grand). [Italian <u>Corteggio</u>, from Court (Latin <u>Cohors</u>, 'retinue')].

LIVING = Here, appointment as Rector of the parish of Queen's Crawley.

ESCHEWED = given up [German <u>Scheuen</u>, 'to shun or avoid'].

DRAFT = In effect, cheque.

REJUVENESCENT = Become young again, like a house newly built [Latin Re-, ´again´ + Juvenescere, ´to grow young´].

ASSIDUOUSLY = Perseveringly [Latin Assidēre, ´to sit down to´; hence Assiduus, ´constantly present´ because always in one´s seat].

AVOCATIONS = Callings; distractions; diversions [Latin A-, ´from´ + Vocāre, ´to call´]. Generally, one´s avocation is one´s business or occupation.

COULOTTE COURTE = Knee-breeches; in effect, the lower half of court dress for men.

DELILAH = The wife of Samson [read the book of Judges in the Bible, chapter 16, verses 4-22, to understand this sentence].

BLOOD = Man (the word indicates high spirits and a fiery disposition).

SUBJUGATED = Subdued; conquered; compelled to submit [Latin Subjugāre, ´to put under the yoke´, and thereafter compel to obey].

TORPID = Without the power of motion [Latin Torpidus, ´numb´].

CHAPTER 46

DISH OF TEA = Here, a special sort of cup, large, with two handles and sometimes no saucer.

BUMPER = Glass of wine, filled to the brim.

HOUSE = Firm [in the sense of an old family firm; such as The House of Fraser, which is run mainly by the Fraser family].

SECEDED = Withdrawn himself; retired [a polite way of saying ´been sacked´, or - as we should put it today - ´made redundant´ [Latin Se-, ´aside´ + Cēdere, ´to go´].

CONNING = Learning; studying [The word Con is a form of the word Can; both come from the Anglo-Saxon Cunnan, ´to know; to know how to do; to be able´].

ACCIDENCE = Inflections; verbs [a form of the word Accidents, meaning the qualities of a word which are not invariable, but change to match other words; for instance, h- indicates a male; He is pronoun for a male, His indicates something belonging to Him - and letters after H- alter according to other words in the sentence. Verbs change similarly, and Latin verbs change more than English verbs now do].

STRAPS TO HIS TROUSERS = Strips of leather at the bottom of each leg, passing under the instep of the boot or shoe. Soldiers wore them, so that they would have seemed grown-up to Georgy.

EUTROPIUS = A Latin reader which was one of ten volumes describing the history of ancient Rome - their author was in Julian´s Persian campaign in AD 363 (Julian being emperor of Rome AD 361 - 363).

USHER = Assistant master [Old French Ussier, ´door-keeper´; hence, one with power to admit people to the presence of the great; eventually, one who walked before the great to make way for them - the great here being the headmaster].

APOTHECARY = Pharmacist [the chemist is the nearest equivalent today; but, at the time of the story, the apothecary was a lower order of physician; a keeper of medicines: from the Greek Apo, ´away´ + Thēkē, ´a chest´ + Tithemi, ´to put´ -

'one who puts [medicines] away in a chest'. The etymology reminds us of the legend printed on paper-bags used by chemists' shops: 'keep all medicines out of the reach of children'].

COPY-BOOKS = Some pupils use copy-books today; but, in case the reader has not used one, we must say that all really good handwriting [calligraphy = 'beautiful writing'] is a copy of the letter-shapes written by a scribe [an expert calligrapher]. The copying is done from exercises written out by a scribe to help student-calligraphers by presenting the difficulties one by one.

PARAGON = Model or pattern - the sort of person others should try to be like; as when one's mother says of someone not very likeable, 'Why aren't you like that?' (and one says to oneself silently, 'Because I wouldn't want to be') [Spanish Para, 'in comparison' + Con, 'with'].

PUBLIC CHARITY LISTS = Lists of those who have contributed (headed by the names of those who have contributed most).

GENTEEL = Well-bred; polite (the word Genteel is used in English sarcastically, because, as Marjorie Challenor says, 'You never call a woman a lady unless you are sure she is not' - and, amazingly, she will not call herself a lady unless she is sure she is not; witness the caller at the door who said, 'Are you the woman who wants a lady to clean for her?' But the French word Gentil is much more assured of itself, and means something very fine indeed; which we borrow in saying of someone we really admire, 'What a gentleman!').

DONKEY-CHAISE = Donkey-cart: a little carriage pulled by a donkey, and entered by a rear door. Low-slung, it was considered the safest owner-driven carriage.

AN ELDER SON = The eldest son got twice the portion of his brothers and sisters in the Biblical tradition [see Deuteronomy 21, verses 15-17].

STARCHED NURSELINGS = Children (wearing garments which positively crackle because of the starch put on them before they were ironed) in the care of a nurse or nursery governess.

SIMPER = Smile in a silly, affected way.

TON = Fashion; manners; breeding.

LAPSED INTO SILENCE = Let the conversation fall away for want of a reply to things said [Latin Lapsus, 'slip, slide or fall;].

ACCEDED = Consented [Latin Accēdere, 'to assent'].

OVERTURES = Proposals [Old French Overture, 'opening'].

MR DOBBIN = ? [Thackeray seems to have made a mistake, for we do not know who Mr Dobbin is].

LUNGING = Holding the rope of a horse as it moves round one [French Longe, 'halter']. The sentence is a little awkward, because the coachman is obviously giving Georgy a treat by letting him sit on the grey pony as the pony is lunged (the G is soft, and has nothing to do with Lungs).

'MY NAME IS NORVAL' = A recitation from John Home's play, Douglas (1754), based on a ballad by Gil Morrice; quoted in A S M Hutchinson's novel, It Happened Like This (1943).

COMPETENCY - Means of livelihood; income [French <u>Competent</u>, from <u>Competer</u>, ´to be sufficient´].

ATTORNEY = Lawyer [French <u>Attorner</u>, ´to transfer´]. The idea is that of someone standing in to transact business on behalf of another because of his greater expertise.

SPECULATION = Buying shares, or in some other way laying out money and risking losing it in the hope of gaining bigger profits than usual [Latin <u>Specula</u>, ´a look-out´ - the speculator is on the look-out for ways of making money].

MAXIM = Rule of conduct [Latin <u>Maxima sententia</u>, ´chief opinion´, or ´best advice´].

FELL INTO ARREAR = Was not paid on time; got behind in payment [French <u>Arriere</u>, from Latin <u>Ad-</u>, ´to´ + <u>Retro</u>, ´behind´].

GARBLED STORY = Story with important bits left out [Arabic <u>Gharbil</u>, ´a sieve´: the story has been sifted, and not all its details have come through].

REMITTANCES = Money orders [Latin <u>Re-</u>, ´away´ + <u>Mittere</u>, ´to send´; ´to send back´ money].

COUNTERMAND = Cancel the order for [Mediaeval Latin <u>Contra-</u>, ´against´ + <u>Mandāre</u>, ´to order´].

´THE PARENTS´ ASSISTANT´ = Stories published in 1796 by Maria Edgeworth (1767-1849).

´SANDFORD AND MERTON´ = A long story for boys published in three volumes between 1783 and 1789 by Thomas Day (1748-1789).

CHAPTER 47

MINDEN = Pronounced to rhyme with linden. In 1759, the Prussians beat the French at Minden (the entrance to the North German plain in north Rhine-Westphalia, 53 miles due south of Bremen on a modern atlas): 53°N, 7°E.

HABITED = Clothed [Latin *Habitus*, ´dress´]. Statues of great men in the seventeenth and eighteenth and even nineteenth centuries showed them wearing the toga; not because they actually did, but simply because it looked so stately.

PASSED AWAY INTO DOWAGERISM = Either the houses looked among houses as withered old women look among people; or the houses are now inhabited by old women. It is an observable fact that, when houses are new, the likeliest purchasers are parents with young children (and these purchasers would have been wealthy, even noble, people). The children grow up, and leave home, and the parents who are left grow old, and eventually are widowed. What a sad look the houses have then!

CASEMENTS = Window-frames.

LINK-BOYS = Boys who carried burning torches made of coarse flax or hemp coated with tar or pitch, to light the way for coach-passengers.

BRASS PLATES = Showing that business houses and professional men have come to do business where formerly only residents were seen; which sometimes means that the square is not so exclusive, but has come down in the world.

REMARK = Distinguish; notice as being different [French *Remarque*, ´notice; observe´].

CLOSE CARRIAGE = A closed carriage, with a roof, doors and windows with curtains; as opposed to an open carriage with low doors only.

MARIANNE CLARKE = Mary Anne Clarke (1776-1852) was mistress (sweet-heart) of the Duke of York from 1803 to 1807.

PETITS APPARTEMENTS = Private rooms.

SALLUST´S HOUSE = Gaius Sallustius Crispus (86-34 BC) was a Roman historian.

COSWAY = Richard Cosway (c1742-1821) painted miniatures [very small portraits] which were ´not only fashionable but the fashion itself´.

EGALITE ORLEANS = In 1792, when French titles were abolished, the Duc d´Orleans [The Duke of Orleans] took the name Philippe Egalite [Philip Equality].

OMBRE = A card-game of the seventeenth and eighteenth centuries, played by three people with forty cards [Spanish Hombre, from Latin Hominem, ´man´].

RECUSANCY = Refusing to conform to the usages of the Church of England [Latin Recusāre, ´to object; to decline to agree with´].

DAUPHINESS = The wife of the Dauphin. The heir to the French crown had other titles, including Lord of Dauphiny (whose crest was a dolphin: dauphin is French for ´dolphin´); for which reason he was known as ´the Dauphin´. The French crown ceased to be from 1830, when there was a revolution.

MADAME DE LA CRUCHECASSEE = Dame Crackpot. Thackeray enjoyed making up funny names for some of his characters (and almost all his invented names give one ideas about the characters to whom they are attached; even Becky Sharp makes one think of a sharp beak - and sharp means dishonest in such a phrase as ´sharp practice´).

SPANISH PLACE = The splendid Roman Catholic church of St James, off Marylebone High Street, in the west end of London.

ARRAS = Tapestry (originally made at Arras, 61 miles south-east by east of Boulogne, in France: 50°N, 3°E).

ST ACHEUL = A Jesuit seminary: that is to say, a college for the training of Roman Catholic priests, run by the Society of Jesus: near Amiens, seventy miles north-by-west of Paris: 50°N, 2°E.

LATIMER/LOYOLA = Hugh Latimer (c 1485-1555) was a notable figure in the Reformation, and a Protestant martyr (though a Cambridge divine; not Oxford, as Thackeray seems to think). Ignatius de Loyola (1491-1556) is the name by which Inigo Lopez de Recalde of Loyola in the Basque province of Guipuzcoa (43°N, 2°W) is best known. At first a page in the court of Ferdinand & Isabella of Spain, he became a soldier, and eventually a religious. He founded the Society of Jesus in 1534.

POST-OBITS = Money lent on a bond to repay when a particular person dies from whose will the borrower has expectations [´I need, say,£1000; and I´ll repay it when my uncle dies. He has left me£3000 in his will´].

TRAVELLERS´ = Club at 196 Pall Mall, established in 1819.

PATE DE FOIE GRAS = A particularly expensive meat-paste made from the liver of geese [literally, ´paste of fat liver´].

ROUT = Multitude [Old French Route, ´company; band´; literally, ´a portion broken off´ - part of the people of a town, but only the best part; the most fashionable part - Latin Rumpere, ´to break´].

NOUS REGARDONS A DEUX FOIS = In effect, ´We must see [such things] more than once [to be certain that they are bad]´: another way of saying, ´I cannot believe my eyes - I don´t believe my eyes´.

SILLERY = High-class wine from the village of Sillery in Champagne ten miles south-east of Rheims (49°N, 4°E), and about sixty miles east of Paris.

ATTACHES = Less important officials on the staff of an ambassador to a foreign court.

CHAPTER 48

DESIDERATUM = Much-wanted thing [Latin].

QUARANTINE = A period of forty days (now a period of indefinite length) during which a ship suspected of infection with a contagious disease is kept in port, and out of bounds to almost everyone [Old French Quarantaine, ´forty days´]; here applied to anything suspected of infection by a contagious disease.

DEAR M--- = Perhaps George Moody, who had been at Charterhouse and at Cambridge with Thackeray.

THE ´HYPOCRITE´ = A play by Isaac Bickerstaffe (c 1735-c 1812).

SLAUGHTER HOUSE SCHOOL = A comic malapropism (mis-saying) for Charterhouse, where Thackeray was a schoolboy. The word School is not part of the name Charterhouse, but Thackeray has put it after Slaughter House for fear of being mis-understood.

BROCADE = Silk stuff decorated with gold and silver, or having raised flowers woven into it. [Spanish Brocado, from French Brocher, ´to prick or emboss´].

COSTUME DE COUR = Dress for wear at court.

CORDONS = Ribbon worn scarfwise, as part of the insignia of a knightly order.

LEVEE DAY = An assembly held in the early afternoon by the Sovereign or his representative, at which only men are received.

DECOLLETEE = In a low-cut dress (literally, ´collarless´).

SULTANAS = Sultan´s wife (here, important women). Not till 1841 did the word begin to mean a small, seedless raisin from Smyrna (now called Izmir) in Turkey: $38°N$, $27°E$.

CHARMANTE = Fascinating.

BRILLIANTS = Diamonds of the finest cut, with faces cut at such an angle as to reflect the light in the most vivid way possible [French Brillant, ´shining´].

REPOSITORY = Place where things are put for safety [Latin Repōnere, ´to put away´ or ´store up´].

DUNNING LETTERS = Letters demanding payment.

NÉE = Born (that is, ´whose surname before she married was´).

MAINTENON = La Marquise de Maintenon (1635-1719) was mistress of Louis XIV from 1669-1719.

POMPADOUR = La Marquise de Pompadour (1721-1764) was mistress of Louis XV.

ROPE-DANCER = What we now call a circus acrobat, who performs feats on a high wire; only rope was used at the time of the story, and the act consisted of pirouetting and balancing rather than anything else.

SWARTHY = Dark-complexioned, and therefore dirty-looking [Old English Sweart, from Latin Sordidus, ´filthy´].

MOUCHOIRS = Handkerchiefs (to wipe away Mouchure, ´mucus´).

GIMCRACKS = Trinkets; small, pretty items of little value.

FIBSTER = A less harsh way of calling someone a liar [probably an abbreviation of Fable, from Fārī, ´to speak´, meaning ´something said´, and eventually ´a fabricated story´].

PIPKIN = An earthenware boiler, or pot in which to boil water [-kin is a diminutive suffix, and a word to which it is added is immediately assigned the idea of littleness; so that a pipkin is a little pipe (and pipes were not necessarily cylindrical, but could mean a large cask or butt)]. Notice the tautology of Thackeray´s adjective here: pipkins were earthenware, so that the adjective is saying the same think twice.

LADY MACBETH = In Shakespeare´s play, Lady Macbeth was bent on murder.

REGAN AND GONERIL = The nasty daughters of King Lear, in another play by Shakespeare.

BALDAQUIN = The canopy above an altar, originally made of rich stuff, with woof [threads which went across] of silk, and warp [threads which went lengthwise] of gold, woven in Baghdad [whose name in Italian was Baldacco]: 33°N, 44°E.

GARE AUX FEMMES = ´Beware of women´.

TÊTE-À-TÊTE = Confidential talk [literally, head to head´, or ´heads together´].

CONGÉ = ´Permission to depart´ accompanied by a bow of farewell - as we say now, the sack; dismissal.

THE REMAINDER IN ONE NOTE = This note is for £1000, and it becomes important to the story in chapter 53, just before the final paragraph.

LIVERYMAN = A man who kept a stable with carriages and horses [Anglo-French Livere, ´handed over´ as an allowance to pay someone to keep horses for the owner].

JOBBED = Hired [dialect Gob, meaning ´a portion´; here, ´a piece of work´].

SPAVIN = Another of Thackeray´s funny names.   Spavin is a disease of horses, making them lame;   so that the name suggests that this liveryman keeps horses in very poor condition.

DRAWINGROOM DAY = Day on which the Sovereign holds a reception in the evening.

HACK CAB = Short for hackney cab [Old Dutch Hackeneye, ´a hacked´ or dock-tailed ´nag´];   a hired cab, pulled by such a horse.

CHAPTER 49

CALUMNIATED = Spoken evil of, falsely [Latin <u>Calumnia</u>, ´false accusation´].

CONTINGENT REVERSION = An arrangement by which an estate returned to the person who borrowed money on the expectation of inheriting it. Lady George has made such an arrangement in effect, by marrying Lord Gaunt´s younger brother. If Lord Gaunt dies childless, Lord Steyne´s title and money will pass to Lady George´s eldest son (for Lord Gaunt is Lord Steyne´s heir at this point in the story). Thus, it could be said that Lord George married Lady George for her money, and that she married him to obtain for the son she hoped to bear the reversion of the Marquisate of Steyne in the contingency (in the event) of Lord Gaunt´s dying childless - ´without issue´.

ALLOCUTION = Speech [Latin <u>Ad-</u>, ´to´ + <u>Loquor</u>, ´to speak´].

VERTU = Value or curiosity [Italian: ´goodness; excellence´]; Thackeray is referring to small antiques, curios and treasures.

BOTTOM = Stamina; strength and vigour.

<u>PLAQUE</u> = Star (a metal plate with the decoration in enamel on it).

<u>PAS</u> = Precedence; the right to walk ahead; pride of place.

YOUNG MARLOW IN THE COMEDY = A character in Goldsmith´s play, <u>She Stoops to Conquer</u>, 1773.

<u>PORTE-COCHERE</u> = Gateway; main entrance: literally, ´carriage-entrance´.

MAGNATES = People of rank or distinction [Latin, ´the great´].

<u>PETITE DAME</u> = Little noblewoman.

RUMOURS = Loud noises; loud expressions of disapproval [Latin <u>Rumor</u>, ´talk´, from the Sanscrit root, <u>Ru-</u>, ´roar´].

CHAPTER 50

TENEMENT = Dwelling; habitation; part of a house forming a separate dwelling; a flat [Latin Tenementum, 'something held' - compare with the word 'householder'; but a tenement would be part of a house, occupied by a Tenant].

MINX = Pert ('cheeky'), wanton ('unrestrained; rude; uneducated') girl [perhaps a corruption of the dialect-word, Minikin, 'lass'].

CARPS = Finds fault unreasonably with; keeps picking on, for no good reason [Latin Carpere, 'to harass; to wear away; to pick or seize on'].

RAILS AT = Scolds; reproaches [French Railler, here, 'to scoff or mock'].

OUTWORKS = Outer defences (the 'little citadel' being Amelia's heart).

SUPPLICATION = Entreaty [the picture is of someone going on her knees to implore, from the Latin Sub-, 'under' + Plicare, 'to fold'].

SUPERSCRIPTION = Address on the envelope [Latin Super-, 'on' + Scribere, 'to write'].

STIPULATED = Laid down the condition [Latin Stipulor, 'to demand a formal promise'].

WONT = Way; habit; custom [Anglo-Saxon Wone, 'to be accustomed'].

HE WAS WONT = He was accustomed.

PARLEYS = conferences; consultations [Mediaeval Latin Parlare, 'to speak' (from which we get the word Parliament, which is known for its much speaking)].

ELATED = Flushed with pride; carried away with enthusiasm [Latin E-, 'out' + Latus, 'carried'].

FAIN = Longing; wishing with all her heart [Anglo-Saxon Faegan, 'joyful'].

BOOTLESS = Unavailing; unrewarded [Anglo-Saxon Bot, 'reparation; amends; gain due'].

BENEFICENT = Doing good [Latin].

CHAPTER 51

ENTRÉE = Entry.

SEMELE = A woman beloved by the god Jupiter [Zeus]. Juno [Hera] persuaded Semele to pray Jupiter to visit her in all the splendour of a god. He did, attended by thunder and lightning, which instantly destroyed her.

TYBURNIA = An exclusive part of the west end of London in the neighbourhood of Portman Square, taking its name from ancient Tyburn (where, till 1783, criminals were hanged).

SOUNDING BRASS AND TINKLING CYMBAL = See the first verse of St. Paul's first epistle to the Corinthians, in the New Testament.

LADY HESTER'S PARTIES = Lady Hester Stanhope (1776-1839) lived with her uncle, William Pitt (who was prime minister from 1783 to 1801, and from 1804 till his death in 1806), as his housekeeper from 1803 till 1806.

MOI QUI VOUS PARLE = In effect, 'I who speak to you now'.

BUMPERS = Glassfuls.

HEELTAP = A little liquor in the bottom of the glass.

BEESWING = The second crust in bottles of port (the crust being formed by sediment in the wine); so-called because of its fragility.

EOTHEN = Alexander William Kinglake (1806-91) wrote a travel book called Eōthen in 1844, describing his tour of the Lebanon in 1835. It was during this tour that he saw Lady Hester.

COMITÉ = Select circle or (as we say now) committee.

SUNDAY SIDE = The delicious, browned outside part of the joint, which would be carved first, when it was brought to the table at Sunday dinner.

AU MIEUX = On the best terms.

PARTIES = Very friendly gatherings.

TRAVELLERS´ = Club at 196 Pall Mall, established in 1819.

ALMACK´S = Assembly rooms in King´s Street, St. James´s, where a committee of great ladies arranged society-balls.

DESCANTING = Discoursing; dwelling (in conversation) [Latin Discantus, ´refrain´ - to say something again and again is said to ´make a song about it´].

PROCURE = Obtain [Latin Procurare, ´to take care of´; to see to something].

ENNUIS = Worries; vexations.

ECUYER = Ring master at a circus [an ecuyer is a professional horseman; so that what Lord Steyne has in mind is really un grand ecuyer, or ´master of the horse´].

TON = Breeding; standing (in the sense of social importance).

REUNIONS = Assemblies; gatherings; receptions; functions.

DRAGOMAN = Interpreter [Arabic Tarjuman].

INTREPID = Undaunted [Latin In-, ´not´ + Trepidus, ´alarmed´].

INGENUE = Artless; unsophisticated; simple; open; frank.

LED CAPTAIN = A hanger-on; someone who was always present, with a view to getting for himself whatever he could.

TRENCHERMAN = Companion [Old French Trencher, ´to cut off´ pieces of bread or meat - Companion itself comes from the Latin Com, ´with´ + Panis, ´bread´, and therefore means one who eats with someone else].

LEER = Glancing sideways with unworthy intent (which might be from ill-will or immodest desire) [Anlo-Saxon Hleor, ´cheek´].

LIGHTED UP = Flamed up; blazed with anger.

PARRIED = Turned his thrusts aside [Latin Parare, ´to keep or ward off´].

RIPOSTED = Attacked successfully after parrying, with a thrust which got ´home´ - which reached its target [Italian Riposta].

NOTES OF HAND = IOU´s; notes acknowledging that one has been lent money, and promising to repay it (usually by a particular date).

VIZIER = Here, private secretary [Arabic Wazir, ´bearer of burdens´; the title of high officers of state in the Turkish Empire].

PARVENUS = Upstarts [´Those who have arrived´ - the idea being that, if one has arrived at a certain level of importance only recently, one cannot be worth much].

LEVY = Raise (money) [Latin Levare, ´to raise´].

EXECUTION = Neither a hanging nor decapitation, but the carrying into effect of a court-sentence to seize the possessions of a debtor [Latin Ex-, ´out´ + Sequor, ´to follow´].

REPRESENTATIONS = Accounts; statements - it would be better, here, to say Misrepresentations, because, of course, they were false statements.

PECUNIARY = Financial [Latin Pecūnia, ´money´].

CAPITALIZED = Used it to trade with (that is, make money with it), and been set up for life [Latin Capitellum, ´a small sum of money´ with which to begin financial transactions].

WAXLIGHTS = Tapers; thin candles.

COMESTIBLES = Articles of food [Latin Comedere, ´to eat´].

GIMCRACKS = Knick-knacks.

PARK HACKS = Ordinary horses for riding in the park.

DEUCE = Devil [Latin Deus, ´god´].

LAFITTE = Claret (red wine) from Chateau Lafitte in Bordeaux [Old French for ´a little clear´, once meaning a yellow or light-red wine; but now meaning dark red].

GIGOTS = Leg-of-mutton sleeves; big, billowing sleeves of rather that shape and size [short for French Des Manches a gigot].

BEDWIN SANDS = Another of Thackeray´s funny names, playing on the word Bedouin [Arabic Badawin; plural of Badawiy, ´desert dweller´].

QUARTO = The book of memoirs expected of every well-born traveller. [Latin In quarto, ´in four´, indicating how the paper is folded for this particular size of book].

BRIAN DE BOIS-GUILBERT = The fierce Knight Templar defeated by the young hero, Ivanhoe, at Ashby-de-la-Zouche in Sir Walter Scott´s first novel (published in 1819).

JANIZARIES = Sultan´s bodyguard of the sons of Christian slaves [Turkish Yeni, ´modern´ + Tsheri, ´militia´], abolished in 1826.

TARBOOSH = Cap of red felt, with a blue tassel, worn by Mohammedans [Arabic Tarbush]; usually called a fez (because such caps were made at the town of Fez in Morocco: 34°N, 5°W).

NARGHILE = Better known as a hookah: a pipe for smoking tobacco, which passes the smoke through water to cool it [Persian Nargil, ´coconut;].

PASTILLE = Cone of aromatic substances, burnt as incense [Latin Pastillus, ´a little loaf´].

YATAGHANS = Turkish word for swords with no hand-guard, and often a double-edged blade.

PASHA = Governor [Turkish].

MARASCHINO = Bottles of a liqueur made from the sour cherry, Marasca, which at this time grew only in Dalmatia (now in western Yugoslavia) on the Adriatic sea: 44°N, 16°E.

PIASTRES = Coins plated with silver [Italian <u>Piastra d´argento</u>].

ZULEIKAH = The heroine of Lord Byron´s poem, ´The Bride of Abydos´, 1813.

CIRCASSIAN = From Circassia, which is known as Kuban; a region noted for the beauty of its people, at the north-west tip of the Caucasus mountains. It was conquered by the Russians in 1864, after which many of its people escaped across the Black Sea to Turkey; but they were making their way to Turkey before that, and many a Circassian girl found her way into slavery in Turkish harems. You will find Kuban in your atlas at, roughly, 37° east. and 45° north - look up Turkey to begin with.

KISLAR AGA = The Sultan´s commander, or chief officer [Turkish].

FIRMAN = Edict or decree; written judgement [Persian <u>Ferman</u>, ´decree´].

DROMEDARIES = Arabian camels, which have one hump (as distinct from the Bactrian camel, which has two) [Latin <u>Dromedarius</u>, from the Greek <u>Dromados</u>, ´running´, from <u>Dramein</u>, ´to run´].

THE MAGIC FLUTE = Mozart´s opera, 1790.

IPHIGENIA = Daughter of Agamemnon and Clytemnestra, who was changed into a deer (as it seemed to her father) when she was about to be sacrificed to Diana at Aulis (facing Chalcis across the Gulf of Euboea, 38°N, 24°E), by the Greeks whose ships the goddess was detaining by contrary winds in revenge for Agamemnon´s slaughter of her stag. In fact, says legend, the goddess (moved by her innocence) spirited her away to Tauris (now known as Crimea, 45°N, 34°E), and put her in charge of her temple.

ANAX ANDRON = ´King of men´ (Homer´s term for Agamemnon).

´BRAVA! BRAVA! BY ---, SHE´D DO IT TOO´ = This statement is recalled by Thackeray, in effect, five and six paragraphs from the end of the last chapter of <u>Vanity Fair</u>, and seems worth noting now.

ARRAS = Tapestry [Arras (50°N, 3°E), a town some sixty miles southeast of Calais, was so noted for its tapestries as to be synonymous for them].

BAGMEN = Commercial travellers, who used to carry bags of samples.

<u>DORMEZ, DORMEZ, CHER AMOURS</u> = ´Sleep, sleep, dear loves´.

<u>AH QUEL PLAISIR D´ETRE EN VOYAGE</u> = ´Ah, what pleasure to be on a voyage´.

OSTLER = Originally, an inn-keeper; at this time, a man charged with the care of horses stabled at an inn [Old French <u>Hostelier</u>].

LE ROSSIGNOL = Not, we may be sure, the ballet by Stravinsky; but probably the story by Hans Anderson (in that he was born in 1805); and Montessu and Noblet were real enough, and danced at the opera house in Paris. Pauline Montessu (1805-1877) danced Lise in the first production of <u>La Fille mal gardee</u>, to new music by Herold in 1828, and took the title-role of <u>Manon Lescaut</u> in 1830. Lise Noblet (1801-1852) created roles in <u>La Sylphide</u> (1832) and <u>La Fille mal gardee</u> (1829): she danced in London in 1821-26. The word <u>Rossignol</u> (like Philomele) means ´nightingale´.

RAVISSANTE = Delightful.

HOURI = Nymph of Paradise - a beautiful woman, forever young [Arabic].

STEPHENS = Catherine Stephens (1794-1882) married the Earl of Essex in 1838, having retired from professional singing.

CARADORI = Maria Caradori (1800-1865) sang in opera, oratorio and on the concert stage.

RONZI DE BEGNIS = Claudina Ronzi (1800-1853) married Giuseppe de Begnis in 1816, and came with him to London in 1822. Lord Mount-Edgecumbe wrote of her, ´With a pretty face and pleasing countenance´ - by which we may suppose him to mean her facial expression - ´she had a voice of great sweetness and flexibility, which she managed with considerable skill and taste. She decidedly excelled in comic parts´.

VESTRIS = Lucia Elizabeth Vestris (1797-1856) ´was extremely bewitching, if not faultlessly beautiful, and endowed with one of the most musical, easy, rich contralto voices ever bestowed on a singer, and retaining its charm to the last´. She sang in opera at Drury Lane and Covent Garden, but preferred a less arduous life than that of professional singing, and managed the Olympic theatre, Covent Garden, and the Lyceum.

RETENUE = Reserve; shyness; self-control; discretion.

TAGLIONI = Marie Sophie Taglioni (1804-1884) reigned supreme at Paris Opera as the greatest dancer of her day. When she danced La Sylphide at Covent Garden in 1832, Thackeray thought her ´the most beautiful and gracious of all dancers´. She retired in 1847.

ECRASED = Eclipsed (literally, ´crushed´).

LINK-MEN = Men who carried a torch made of tow (coarse flax) and tar, to light passengers to and from their vehicles.

INTERLOCUTOR = The person who spoke with him [Latin Inter-, ´between´ + Loquor, ´to speak´].

CHAPTER 52

EMULATION = Trying hard to do as well as others do [Latin <u>Aemūlarie</u>, ´to compete with´].

PUGILISTIC EXERCISES = Fist-fights [Latin <u>Pugil</u>, ´boxer´].

CONTIGUOUS = Next (literally, ´touching´) [Latin <u>Contingere</u>].

EXTERN = Outer [Latin <u>Externus</u>].

LAICS = Men other than clerics (or clergymen) [Greek <u>Laos</u>, ´people´].

PRELATES = Priests of high rank, such as bishops [Latin <u>Pre-</u>, ´before´ + <u>Lātus</u>, ´carried´]. You may have seen the Pope, on television, carried above the heads of the crowd; which will give you an idea of the reason for this word.

RACING CALENDAR = Book giving the dates of race-meetings [Latin <u>Calendārium</u>, ´account-book´, from <u>Calendae</u>, ´the first day of the month´, when payment was due; hence, a table of months and days].

BLUBBERED = Wept till her face was swollen.

TRUMP = A good fellow [contracted from Triumph].

FAG = In effect, his servant (it was the custom at public schools for the youngest boys to act as servants for the most senior boys).

<u>PROTEGÉ</u> = One under the patronage or protection of another.

ASTLEY´S = A circus at Lambeth from 1770.

FEE-SIMPLE = Estate in lands or tenements belonging to the owner and his heirs for ever. Mayfair has been the most fashionable part of London for many years.

CURTAILED = Lessened [Latin <u>Curtus</u>, ´short´].

PUMPING = Putting artful questions, to extract information which the other person is hardly aware of imparting.

ELEVEN HUNDRED AND TWENTYFIVE POUNDS = Not quite the sum of money which Becky possessed. The one note mentioned in the antepenultimate paragraph of chapter 48 we know from the sixth paragraph from the end of chapter 53 to be worth £1,000; and the rest of the money mentioned in chapter 48 is ´a hundred and fifty pounds in small notes´.

FOUR COVERS DAILY = Four places laid (in other words, she had guests, as befitted a woman of importance).

EXPOSTULATED = Asked with some urgency [Latin <u>Expostulāre</u>, ´to demand vehemently´].

EXEMPLARY = Worthy of imitation by others [Latin <u>Exemplum</u>, ´model; pattern´].

<u>PREVENANCES</u> = Attentions; kindnesses.

CHAPTER 53

PLACENS UXOR = Charming wife [Latin].

BARRED INTO A SPUNGING-HOUSE = Locked up in a house where people arrested for debt were kept by a bailiff for twentyfour hours to give their friends opportunity to pay off the debt.

PROMISSORY NOTE = What we call an IOU, promising to pay a specific sum of money, either on a specified date or on demand.

EN PERMANENCE = Permanently (if you think of it, people normally put bottles of wine and so forth away in a cupboard, and get them out only when needed; but, at Mr Moss´s, they were left out).

CORNICES = Ornamental mouldings running round a room, mirror or window [Italian].

WAFERS = Small discs of flour and gum (or gelatine) for sealing letters, attaching papers, or receiving the impression of a seal (like sealing wax) [Middle Low German Wâfel, ´waffle´].

MON PAUVRE CHER PETIT = My poor little darling.

MONSTRE = Probably short for Monstre d´homme (´Brute of a man´), as Rawdon was used to being called for fun.

BIEN MAUVAISE MINE = A thoroughly shady look (the look of a rascal).

SENTOIT LE GENIEVRE = Reeking of gin.

VENTRE A TERRE = At full speed.

TRISTE VISITE CHEZ MON ONCLE = Sad visit to ´my uncle´ = the pawnbroker.

CE CHER ONCLE = That [same] dear uncle.

FOISON = Plenty [Latin Fūsiō, ´outpouring;´].

MON PAUVRE PRISONNIER = My poor prisoner [of a husband].

TABLE D´HÔTE = Dining table (where everyone sat, as opposed to the private tables available for the highest-paying patrons of superior hotels).

CAROUSING = Drinking [German _Gar ouse_ (_trinken_), ´(to drink) right out´ - to drink all the liquor that remained to be drunk].

THE WRETCHED WOMAN = Here, contemptible;   degraded [Anglo-Saxon _Wrecca_, ´outcast´].

SERPENTS = Ornaments so shaped [Greek _Herpein_, ´to creep´;   hence, Latin _Serpens_, ´creeping thing´].

BAUBLES = Trinkets [Old French _Baubel_, ´toy´].

BULLY = Here, one who lives on the earnings of an immoral woman.

MULTIFARIOUS = Consisting of many different things [Latin _Multifarius_, ´many and varied´].

TRUMPERY = Showy but worthless finery [Frency _Tromperie_, ´wile or fraud´].

NOTE FOR A THOUSAND POUNDS = Mentioned in chapters 48 [Everyman edition, p 486] and 52 [E ed, p 526].

LAUDANUM = Alcoholic tincture of opium (the dried juice of certain poppy-heads grown mainly in China, India and Iran, containing a number of medicinal substances of which the most important is morphine).   Theophrastus Bombastus von Hohenheim (1493-1541) invented the name Laudanum for a chemical compound whose chief ingredient was suspected of being opium, and the name Paracelsus for himself.   He worked principally at Basle and Salzburg.   Laudanum was a sleeping draught, and Rebecca´s thought is to take an over-dose.

CHAPTER 54

BARKING BUTCHER AND TUTBURY PET = Prize-fighters - bare-knuckle boxers, who used to sustain terrible injuries.

WHITE-WASHED = Cleared of responsibility for paying his debts by a legal process which prevented him contracting any more (which meant that he could not borrow money, but had to pay in cash for every transaction).

WRAP A BALL IN THE NOTE = The sort of ball discharged by a musket; a ball of lead - the word 'bullet' means 'a little ball' in this sense [Latin Bulla, 'bubble or knob'].

AUGURING = Sensing the coming of [Latin Augur, 'soothsayer' - a Roman official who predicted the future chiefly from the observation of birds (and soothsayer comes from the Anglo-Saxon Soth, 'truth')].

LIVERIES = Uniforms; the distinctive clothing in which the male servants of some people of position were clad [French Livree, 'given out', as a uniform would be; from Latin Liberāre, 'to pay'].

SILENUS = The henchman or attendant of Bacchus, the Roman god of wine and revelry.

DISHEVELLED = Having one's hair disordered [Old French Descheveler, 'putting one's hair out of order', from Des-, 'to deprive of the character or nature of' + Chevel, 'hair'].

ENJOINED = Ordered [Latin Injungere, 'to impose a duty on'].

PUBLICAN = Inn-keeper [Latin Publicus, 'general or ordinary'; probably from Poplicus, 'people'; the keeper of a people's house].

BELL'S LIFE = Probably short for Bell's Sporting Life, which reported what some people call sport, including fisticuffs.

QUOD = Prison (slang abbreviation for 'quadrangle', for the four walls of a cell or exercise yard).

SHINTY = Quarrel, row or commotion. We now spell that meaning of the word Shindy, but it began as the game still played in Scotland, which involved cries of, ´Shin you!´, or, ´Shin ye!´. Another aspect is spelt Shindig, meaning a party at which occurs some wild or ´shin-scraping´ dancing (as in ´Knees up, Mother Brown´).

TRISTE = Doleful; gloomy.

CHAPTER 55

PLY = Press on; to use diligently [the aphetic (or ´worn-down´) version of Apply, ´to put into operation´].

MADEMOISELLE FIFINE = Compare the spelling of the name in Becky´s letter in chapter 53 [E ed, p 534].

PET = Ill humour (thoroughly bad temper) at not being made enough of.

MORE EXALTED PERSONS = Such as Louis-Philippe, who (as elder son of the Duc d´Orleans) fled from Paris in 1793.

FESTIN = Banquet.

FIRE-IRONS = Tongs, pokers, &c.

CHIMNEY-GLASSES = Mirrors over the fireplaces.

AFFREUSEMENT VOLE = Dreadfully robbed.

CHINTZ = Cotton cloth printed with flowers in at least five different colours [Persian Chinz, ´spotted or stained´,]: the best is now printed in twenty-three colours.

MARASCHINO = Liqueur made from the sour cherry, Marasca, which at this time grew only in Dalmatia (now in western Yugoslavia) on the Adriatic sea: 44°N, 16°E.

SUGAR-LOAF = Conical in shape, as blocks of refined sugar used to be.

HORSE HAW-HAW = Loud, coarse laugh.

PIGEON-MATCH = Shooting live pigeons released from a cage.

CROSS = As we should put it, it was ´fixed´ - the result decided beforehand, and therefore not a fair fight.

DRAG = Private stage-coach, with seats inside and on top.

FILES = Here, shrewd followers [French <u>Fils</u>, ´son´].

DEMIREPS = Women of doubtful reputation [from the ´demimonde´, where people who are not entirely respectable are only half-acknowledged, even though they appear to be wealthy enough: short for <u>Demi-reputation</u>].

MEERSCHAUM PIPE = Pipe of fine white clay (silicate of magnesium) found on the shore, looking like petrified sea-foam [German for ´sea-foam´].

SCORE = Debt (´scored´ or written up on a slate).

PRINTS = Press; newspapers.

PONY = The sum of £25 (which was about the price of the animal then).

<u>PEKIN</u> = Civilian [French <u>Pequin</u>].

<u>RENCONTRE</u> = Encounter; confrontation.

<u>DAME D´HONNEUR</u> = Lady-in-waiting.

GUAVA JELLY = Jelly (spread on bread and butter) made from the fruit of a small tree of the myrtle family, found in Guiana (now known in part as Surinam, South America: 5°N, 55°W).

CHAPTER 56

COLLEGIAN = Member of a college (the implication being, one who did so well in his examinations as to be granted a fellowship to enable him to stay and study at Oxford or Cambridge for the rest of his life).

INVEIGH = To rail, or utter criticisms [Latin _Invehor_, 'to attack with words'].

SUPERCILIOUS = From the Latin _Super-_, 'above' + _Cilia_, 'eyebrows': picture someone raising his eyebrows, and you will see what Mr Osborne meant.

DOGS = Slang for men of little worth.

OR = Of gold [Latin _Aurum_, 'gold', which became French _Or_].

COCKADE = A ribbon or knot of ribbon worn in the hat: perhaps a black leather rosette, badge of the House of Hanover (the royal family), as worn by officers' servants. Different colours proclaimed different nationalities.

FEATHERS = Usually of ostrich, worn in the hat by way of ornament.

LAWN = Fine linen [from Laon in France (49.5°N, 3.5°E), 90 miles NE of Paris].

NATTY = Spruce; smart; trim [akin to 'neat'].

MOROCCO = Goat's leather, originally from Morocco (33°N, 5°W, in Africa).

HARDBAKE = Sweet made with boiled sugar or treacle with blanched almonds.

WEST'S FAMOUS CHARACTERS = Made by William West of cardboard for toy theatres.

RUM-SHRUB = Lemon or orange juice, with sugar and rum [Arabic _Shurb_, 'drink'].

BUNGLERS = Those who perform without skill [akin to 'bang; beat' - who go through the motions of business, but do not deliver fully wrought products].

AFFECTED = Assigned; appointed [French _Affecté_, in the military sense (which meant 'posted')].

113

SEDULITY = Diligence; assiduity; perseverance; steady industry [Latin Sēdulus; from Sedēre, 'to sit', with the idea of settling oneself to a task]: what we now call 'stickability'.

ORRERY = A mechanism representing the movement of the planets round the sun, by clockwork (after Charles Boyle, Earl of Orrery, for whom one was first made).

DESCANTED = Discoursed; talked; enlarged; 'warbled' [Latin Dis-, 'apart' + Cantus, 'a song': the idea is of one going on and about a topic to the point of 'making a song and dance about it'].

EUTROPIUS = Roman historian who took part in Julian's Persian campaign in AD 363: his simple Breviarium ab urbe condita was an early reader for pupils in grammar schools [and 'grammar school' till the 1940's always meant 'Latin-grammar school'].

CONVERSAZIONI = Meetings (generally in the evening) for conversation; receptions [Italian].

AΘHNH = Pallas Athene, goddess of wisdom [Greek].

ARISTOS = The best [Greek].

OPTIMUS = The best [Latin].

TRES BIEN = Very good [French].

PLUSH SMALLS = Velvet or velveteen breeches.

THRUM = Play coarsely or unskilfully on a stringed instrument [akin to Drum and Strum].

TOADY = Short for 'toad-eater', meaning someone so servile ['slavish'] that he would descend to any indignity to please his master.

D'AVANCE = In advance.

DRAG - Long carriage, drawn by four horses, uncovered, and seated round the sides.

LAQUAIS DE PLACE = Footman.

CRACKERS = Small fireworks [not biscuits, which were known at this time and for many years afterwards as 'cracknel'].

CHAPTER 57

EOTHEN = See the note near the beginning of Chapter 51.

SABLES = Mourning clothes [Sable is the heraldic word for Black].

LATUDE'S BEARD AND WHISKERS = Henri Masers de Latude (1725-1805) was a French artillery officer who tried to win Madame de Pompadour's favour by revealing a plot (of his own devising) to poison her. He was imprisoned in the Bastille, when he made three daring but futile attempts to escape. His pet mouse (a wild mouse) was as much a legend as Bruce's spider.

TRENCK = Frederick the Great imprisoned first Franz, Baron Trenck (1711-49), and then his cousin Freidrich (1726-94); the first at Spielburg (the Hapsburg state prison in Brno: 49°N, 17°E: in Moravia, 1742-1855), and the second at Magdeburg, 52°N, 12°E (in west central East Germany, on the river Elbe, south-west of Berlin). The reference could be to either.

CUTCHERRY = The court-house [Hindi Kachahri] or public office.

BRANDY-PAWNEE = Brandy and water [Hindi Pani, 'water'].

CUDDY-TABLE = Supper table [Irish Cuid Oidhche, 'evening portion'].

PAS = First place; place of honour.

SINGLE-STICK = Fencing with a stick (instead of a sword) provided with a hand-guard or basket to prevent injury.

CHAPTER 58

CHILLUM = The part of a hookah (or elaborate Indian pipe, which sent the smoke through water to cool it) containing the tobacco [Hindi <u>Chilam</u>].

POST-CHAISE = Two-wheeled carriage with a hood, driven by postilions, hired to take passengers from one railway station to another (competing lines having stations at the same town going to different destinations; for instance, in travelling from London to Poyle, one would leave the Southern Railway at Staines, and drive to the Great Western Railway on the other side of the town) or from one stage of their journey to another.

SHIRKING = Moving silently (which is what we mean when we say that we ´stole away´).

BLUCHERS = Strong, leather half-boots, named after Field-Marshal Gebhard Leberecht von Blücher (1742-1819), who helped the Duke of Wellington to defeat Napoleon.

WELLINGTONS = Not the rubber boots we wear, but a high boot of leather, covering the knee in front, and cut away behind the knee; after the first Duke of Wellington (1769-1852).

VOLLEY OF BAD LANGUAGE = An outpouring [of oaths] in rapid succession [Latin <u>Volāre</u>, ´to fly; to let fly´].

FLACCID = Flabby; drooping; soft [Latin <u>Flaccidus</u>, ´languid; feeble´]. The pronunciation is a hard C followed by a soft C, as in ´accident´.

MOREEN = A stout woollen (or woollen and cotton) material, plain or watered (that is, having a wavy appearance on its surface) [French <u>Moire</u>, from Mohair, or cloth made from the hair of the Angora goat].

CHAY = Short for Chaise: a two-wheeled carriage with a collapsible hood [French, from <u>Chaise</u>, ´chair´]. The pronunciation, ´shays´, made people think that the word used Shay or Chay for one chaise.

EXTANT = In being; not destroyed or lost [Latin, ´outstanding´].

INDUCTED = Led or brought [Latin <u>Indūcere</u>, ´to lead or bring in´].

BUXOM = Meek, gracious, obliging [Anglo-Saxon Buhsom, 'compliant; obedient'; from Bugan, 'to bend; to bow']. There is hardly a word so well-known, whose actual meaning is so little known. Most people would interpret the word as meaning, 'attractive - seems like a nice girl'; so that we might re-interpret it as healthy, cheerful, lively, brisk, vigorous; but its real meaning is based on a profound hope on the part of humanity (male and female) that woman will prove willing to do what she is asked. If she does, she is buxom in the true sense.

EJACULATORY = Here, sudden [Latin Ejaculāri, 'to throw out', as one 'flings out' a hint]. The chances are, that it was not the breaks which were ejaculatory, but the short sentences which the Sedley trio flung into those breaks.

FROCK-COAT = A coat as long in front as it was behind (unlike a tail-coat, which was short in front) [Latin Floccus, 'a flock (or lock) of wool'].

'FATHERLESS FANNY' = A novel published in 1819 for the edification of the lower classes, and read by weaker minds among the middle class.

'THE SCOTTISH CHIEFS' = A novel published in 1810 by Jane Porter (1776-1850).

FÊTES = Rejoicings.

GRANDES EAUX = 'Great waters' (in other words, Amelia was in floods of tears whenever she was happy. Such tears are called tears of joy; but it is said that, in fact, these are the tears of grief which we shed only when we feel safe in expressing past sorrows).

BREAD-AND-BUTTER = Schoolgirlish.

EXTORTED = Squeezed out; wrung [Latin Extorquēre, 'to twist out; to force away'].

REPINE = To show discontent [Latin Repungere, 'to sting again']; to fret' to murmur.

CHAPTER 59

QUIZZING GLASSES = Monocles (which were raised to one's weaker eye to reinforce a look at someone or something).

OGLE = Cast side-glances at, to attract their attention [Low German <u>Oegeln</u>, 'to eye'].

VESTS = Waistcoats (which is what Americans mean by the word now) [Latin <u>Vestis</u>, 'a garment'].

SWELL = Well-dressed, fashionable man.

<u>**PERSICOS APPARATUS**</u> = In effect, Persian pomp or splendour; for Jos travelled in the style of an Eastern potentate [the reference will be found in Horace's <u>Odes</u>, I.38].

HIEING = Hastening [Anglo-Saxon <u>Higian</u>, 'to strive; to pant'].

LIVID = The colour of lead (the metal) [Latin <u>Lividus</u>, 'blueish'].

GIZZARD = Entrails after being cooked [Latin <u>Gigēria</u>, 'the entrails of poultry'], especially the third and principal stomach in birds, which is usually very thick and muscular.

CONFIDANTE = Friend entrusted with secrets [Latin <u>Con</u>, 'with' + <u>Fĩdere</u>, 'to trust']. The E at the end reveals the friend to be female: it must be omitted to designate a male friend.

CONSUMPTIVE = Ill with phthisis (or pulmonary tuberculosis), which caused the patient to waste away - to get thinner and weaker.

DESDEMONA = The heroine of Shakespeare's play, <u>Othello</u> (1604).

MIRANDA = The heroine of Shakespeare's play, <u>The Tempest</u> (1611)

BENGALEE = Man from Bengal (now divided into west Bengal, in India, with a population of 26,000,000, and east Bengal, 23°N, 90°E, which comprises east Pakistan, with a population of 43,000,000); not necessarily a native or a coloured man.

PILAUS = Rice cooked with fat, butter, meat or fish, with spices and raisins, &c [Persian Pilāw, which the Turks pronounce ´peelaff´].

JOBBED = Hired.

WAFERS = Small, adhesive discs of paste.

LOCATAIRES = Lodgers.

BAROUCHE = Carriage with a collapsible top, driven from the box or by postilions, with four or six horses [German dialect Barutsche, from Late Latin Birotus, ´two-wheeled´].

COT = Dwelling [Anglo-Saxon Cot, ´chamber´]. The idea of ´humble´ is inseparable from the word, which became cottage, and, in German, indicated a hut; so that Miss Clapp was following the English tradition of adding an adjective to express what the word already signified (compare the present-day ´pre-programmed´; ´foot-pedal´; and - via the BBC - ´new innovation´).

ODIOUS = Hateful; offensive [Latin Odiōsus].

SERVILITY = Slavish deference [Latin Servīlis, ´concerning slaves´].

FULSOME = Extravagant to the point of being nauseating - making the hearer feel slightly sick [linked to Anglo-Saxon Ful, in the sense of ´foul´, ´over-ripe´].

SYCOPHANT = Flatterer.

USAGE = Treatment [Latin Ūtor ´to use´].

PETTISHNESS = Fretfulness; peevishness; irritability [possibly linked to Latin Petulantia, ´wantonness; wilfulness´].

CHAPTER 60

PENURY = Poverty (Thackeray is being sarcastic, as if to say, ´They think it poverty, but we ordinary mortals think it riches´) [Latin P̄en̄ūria, ´want´].

HAMMERCLOTH = Cloth placed over the driver´s seat, with coat of arms where it overhung the seat [Dutch <u>Hemel</u>, ´top of a coach; cover; canopy´], protected in wet weather by a waterproof sheet.

LONGTAIL = Any animal with a long tail (originally a dog or horse whose tail had not been docked: unbelievable as it must seem, it is not many years ago that dogs and horses were regarded as unfinished unless they had had such amputation). Georgy is alluding cheekily to the Major´s horsy face; and he must indeed have had one or Thackeray would have named him differently [Major <u>Who?</u>].

OTIOSITY = Leisure (with a hint at uselessness) [Latin Ōtium, ´rest; ease´].

<u>**AMI DE LA MAISON**</u> = Family friend.

LACS = Hundreds of thousands of rupees (silver coins worth what 10p would have been worth then; about 2) [Sanskrit <u>Laksha</u>).

<u>**ENTRÉES**</u> = Made dishes (courses assembled from several ingredients, generally including recooked poultry) served between other courses or before the joint of meat.

<u>**MUTATO NOMINE**</u> = Short for, <u>Mutato nomine</u> (´Change the name [or the hero/heroine]´), <u>de te fabula narratur</u> (´and this could be your story´ (or, as we might say today, ´this is <u>your</u> life´).

CIRCUIT = The succession of criminal courts (called Assizes) visited by High Court judges and barristers in the course of a legal session, or year, to try cases referred to them by lower courts [Latin <u>Circum</u>, ´round´ (adverb) + <u>Īre</u>, ´to go´].

MRS PICE = Regrettable as it seems to unsympathetic temperaments, Thackeray loves revealing character (or the way in which he sees character in his mind´s eye) through names. Pice were East Indian coins worth half a farthing (that is, not taking into account the loss of value of our money during 150 years, a twentieth of our penny): so Mrs Pice did not amount to much.

USING OURSELVES = Pronounced with a double-S sound, to mean ´getting used to´, or ´accustoming ourselves to´.

VISITING-BOOK = Not, as one might think, the book signed by visitors on their first call, but a book listing those whom one intended to visit, taken with one in the carriage [Latin Visitāre, ´to see often´].

ARTLESS = Simple; natural; unaffected; sincere.

FURLOUGH = Leave of absence [German Verlaub, ´leave; permission (to be absent)´].

INDIAN DANDIES = Dandies [smartly dressed young men] from India; dandies who worked there, but were not of Indian blood.

TEARING CABS = Fast-moving cabriolets, or public coaches so-called because of the way in which they moved - which was not steady [French Cabrioler, ´to caper; to skip like a goat´, from Latin Caper, ´goat´].

BUCK = Dandy [from thought of the male deer or rabbit, gleaming with what the Bible calls ´the pride of life´].

DRAWING-ROOM = The formal reception of a company of people in the evening at Court.

CHAPTER 61

SECOND STOREY = A storey is the space between floors <u>not counting the</u> <u>ground-floor</u>; so the first floor is always upstairs, and the second storey would be reached by a second flight of stairs. Only servants slept up as many stairs as that [Old French <u>Estorer</u>, ´to build´].

UTILITY = Usefulness [Latin <u>Ūtilis</u>, ´useful´].

THE BLACK ARK = The coffin (made of dark wood) [Latin <u>Arca</u>, ´coffin; chest; coffer; prison´].

LURKS = Moves unobtrusively about [cf ´shirking´, Everyman edition, p 583].

SPUTTERING = Akin to the verbs Spout and Spit: to sputter is to speak so rapidly as to emit saliva. The candle sputtered probably because the tallow [´animal fat melted and clarified´] contained tiny drops of moisture.

JUDAH/SIMEON/BENJAMIN = Sons of Jacob [see the Book of Genesis, chapter 29, verses 33-35; chapter 35, verses 16-18].

RUBBER = A game of whist [card game for four, played with a full pack; so-called because the players must be ´whist´, or silent]. Strictly, a rubber is three games of whist (in practice, two, if the same people win the first two games) or five (in which case, whoever won three would make further games unnecessary). The word Rubber could be applied to backgammon, cribbage or bowls when they were played as the best two out of three games, or the best three out of five [its origin is unknown]; but ´a hand´ means ´a share of cards´, so whist must be meant here.

QUERULOUS = Plaintive [Latin <u>Querulus</u>, ´complaining´].

FILIAL = Befitting a son or daughter toward a parent [Latin <u>Fīlialis</u>, ´pertaining to a <u>Fīlius</u> (son) or <u>Fīlia</u> (daughter)´].

BOOTLESS Pointles; to no avail; without advantage [Anglo-Saxon <u>Bot</u>, ´reparation; amends´ - from which we get the word Better].

JOINTURE = Property jointly owned for the benefit of the survivor (as when a couple say, ´The house is in both our names´).

DIRGE = Song of mourning [from Psalm 5, verse 8, which began the antiphon in the Roman Office of the Dead in Latin, 'Dirige, Domine, viam meam' - 'Direct, O Lord, my way'].

ASPERITY = Harshness; roughness [Old English Asprete, 'bitter coldness'].

YOUNKERS = Young fellows [Dutch Jonk heer, 'young sir'].

EXECUTOR = Someone appointed to see to it that the last will and testament of the deceased is indeed carried out as he wished [Latin Ex-, 'out' + (S)equi, 'to follow'].

PAUPER = Someone dependent on charity [Latin Pauper, 'poor'].

VICTUALS = Provisions [Late Latin Victualia, 'forms of nourishment']: pronounced VITTLES.

PANTECHNICON = A place where all kinds of manufactured articles were collected, and displayed for sale; a warehouse (in our day, a van) for the collection of furniture [Greek Pan-, 'all' + Techne, 'art'].

SABLES = Mourning garments.

THE FOUNDLING = The chapel of the Foundling Hospital [see chapter 12].

FLACCID = Limp; flabby [Latin Flaccus, 'loose; flagging']. In saying it, remember to make the first C hard, and the second C soft, as in Accident.

ARBOUR = A shady recess made with boughs intertwined, or climbing plants; usually with a garden seat [Latin Herbarium, 'herb-garden'].

DROLL = Amusing (in the sense of 'funny-peculiar'); odd [French Drôle, 'strange; ludicrous'].

QUE VOULEZ-VOUS? = 'What would you expect?'

DRYSALTER = Dealer in chemical products used in the arts; in drugs, gum, sauces, pickles (which, being in jars or bottles, did not make your hands wet or sticky); formerly one who traded in preserved meats (which had been cured, or packed in salt and then dried out).

BLUE = Learned; pedantic [after the stockings worn by the botanist Benjamin Stillingfleet (1702-71) to Mrs Vesey's 'evening assemblies without card-games' at Bath, where the conversation was distinctly high-toned].

MRS SOMERVILLE = Mary Somerville (1780-1872) wrote The Connection of the Physical Sciences (1834) and other works. The Oxford college is named after her.

THE ROYAL INSTITUTION = Founded by Fellows of the Royal Society, with a view to applying science to 'the useful purposes of life' (1799). Splendid lectures to children are given at Christmas time, at 21 Albemarle Street, London W1.

EXETER HALL = In the Strand (not opened till 1831, and therefore an anachronism ['something which had yet to be'] at this point in the story [Greek Ana-, 'backwards' + Chronos, 'time'].

CLAVERS = Gossip; idle chatter [Scottish]. The word reveals Thackeray's estimate of the value of what were intended to be clever conversations by those who took part in them.

FIDDLE-FADDLE = Trifling talk.

SLIPSLOP = Loose or trifling talk.

TERGIVERSATION = Turning one's back on a position previously favoured [Latin Tergum, 'the back' + Versor, 'to turn'].

EPRIS = Smitten; fallen (in love); taken (with her) - all military expressions concerning the battle of the sexes.

TON = Breeding (by which Mrs Hollyock means a haughty manner).

CHAPTER 62

GODDEM = Presumably, the characteristically English exclamation which was uttered at everything seen and heard abroad [Old French <u>Godon</u> meant ´Englishman´].

BRAMAH DESKS = Invented by Joseph Bramah (1748-1814) - the first syllable of whose name rhymes with ram: a small, portable box made at this time by Messrs Bramah & Prestage of Piccadilly can be seen at the Victoria & Albert Museum: with one of Bramah´s pick-proof locks; it opens to provide a leather-covered writing slope, ink wells, pen rest, various spaces and even a secret drawer or two. Desks on a larger scale were made, and had the appearance of trunks.

<u>TRENTE-ET-QUARANTE</u> - Card-game sometimes called <u>rouge et noir</u>, of which we hear much in the next chapters: it had a banker, and four diamond-shaped spots on the table (two red, two black) on which bets were placed.

IMPERIALS = Cases designed to be carried on a carriage roof.

<u>FEMMES DE CHAMBRE</u> = Ladies´ maids (a distinctly superior type).

COURIERS = Travelling servants who went ahead to make all arrangements for a trouble-free journey. Remember, there were no telephones. These servants have either been ahead, and returned to travel with their employers, or will shortly precede their masters once the first leg of the journey is over.

BRITZKA = Large vehicle introduced from Hungary in 1818, which could be converted into a sleeping compartment by raising the sides and hood [diminutive of Polish <u>Bryka</u>, ´goodswagon´].

FOURGON = Big coach with much space for luggage, and an enlarged box-seat, in which footmen, valets and maidservants (often with an armed escort) in the charge of a courier went ahead of their employers to unpack and get rooms ready [French, ´baggage-wagon´].

<u>A QUI CETTE VOITURE LA?</u> = ´Whose is that carriage?´

<u>C´EST A KIRSCH, JE BENSE</u> - <u>JE L´AI VU TOUTE A L´HEURE</u> - <u>QUI BRENOIT DES SANGVICHES DANS LA VOITURE</u> = ´It´s for Kirsch, I think. I just saw him (or, I saw him just now), taking sandwiches in the coach´ [the heavy pronunciation reveals the speaker to be German].

125

POLYGLOT = 'Many-tongued'; in many languages.

NABOB = Here, one who has acquired great wealth in the East, and spends it ostentatiously [Hindi Nawwab].

IMPERIALS = Here, carriage-roofs (from the type of case designed to be carried there) [French Imperiales, 'the top or outside of a coach'].

NOUS ALLONS AVOIR UNE BELLE TRAVERSÉE = 'We're going to have a good crossing'.

HERR GRAF LORD VON SEDLEY NEBST BEGLEITUNG AUS LONDON = Count Lord Sedley and company of London.

POSTILLIONS = Rider on the nearside horse leading four, or of two pulling a carriage (traditionally in perpetual danger of being struck by lightning, for reasons which are not entirely clear).

BANDANNA = A tie-dyed handkerchief [Hindi Bandhnu, 'tie-dying'; that is, twisting cloth, and tying pieces of string round it to prevent its untwisting while immersed in a vat of dye. It dries out pleasantly pied].

GALIGNANI'S ADMIRABLE NEWSPAPER = Galignani's Messenger was a Parisian publication advocating cordiality between France and England, published daily for Englishmen abroad. It was founded by Giovanni Antonio Galignani (died in 1821), but much improved by his sons, John Anthony (1796-1873) and William (1798-1882). It ran from 1814 till 1884 under that name, and as The Daily Messenger till 1904. Thackeray calls it 'piratical' because all its news was quoted from other publications.

HIS TRANSPARENCY = The German for 'Serence Highness' is Durchlaucht. Thackeray is pretending to read Durchlassend, 'transparent'.

BULBUL FACTION = The party whose allegiance was to a young woman pictured as one of a species of thrush sometime referred to as 'the nightingale of the East'.

PUMPERNICKERL = Weimar, which Thackeray knew as a young man. The Oxford Book of Literary Anecdotes has a delightful passage by Thackeray's daughter describing the visit which he made there with her when he was much older, and what it meant to him [see pages 302-306].

TABLE D'HÔTE = Common table [host's table'] with set meals.

JOHANNISBERGER = The finest and most expensive of Rhenish wines, grown on the estate of the Bishop of Fulda, above the village of Geisenheim, some fourteen miles west-south-west of Mainz 50°N, 8°E (itself about 35 miles west-south-west of Frankfurt) in Germany. The vineyard lay within the grounds of the Benedictine monastery of St John the Baptist (which is what 'Johannisberger' means).

SCHINKEN - Ham (think of the English word Shank, as in 'Shanks's pony' - it means the shin, from knee to ankle, now; but originally meant thigh, which is where ham strictly comes from).

BRATEN = Roast [from the French Braise, 'hot charcoal' - think of Brazier, by which the watchman sat].

KARTOFFELN = Potatoes.

MACAROON = A small cake or biscuit containing ground almonds [Italian Maccarrone; originally ´a mixture of flour, cheese and butter´].

ESPIEGLERIE = Mischievousness.

BAULK = Thwart;   deny [Old English Balca, ´ridge;   strip of land left unploughed´].

GAST-ROLLE = Guest-star [German].

SCHROEDER-DEVRIENT = Wilhelmina Schroder-Devrient (1804-1860) sang the part of Pamina in Mozart´s opera, The Magic Flute, when she was 17 years old.   ´The freshness of her well-developed soprano, her purity of intonation and certainty of attack, astonished the public´, says Grove´s Dictionary (1927, IV, 577).

LOGE = Box.

BLASÉ = Sophisticated;   worldly wise;   behaving as though he ´knows it all´.

NICHTS, NICHTS, MEIN FLORESTAN = ´Nought, nought, my Florestan´ (or, ´Nothing, nothing´).

DIE SCHLACHT BEI VITTORIA = ´The battle of Vittoria´ was the sub-title for the orchestral work entitled, ´Wellington´s Victory´, which was first performed on 8 December 1813, and dedicated to ´The Prince Regent of England´.

WHITE DUCK TROUSERS = Trousers made of strong, untwilled (that is, unribbed) fabric [Dutch Doeck, ´linen´].

ASPIC OF PLOVER´S EGGS = A clear, savoury jelly containing the small but delicately tasty eggs of the ´rain bird´ [Latin Pluvia, ´rain´], which nests in meadows, on river banks, and on the seashore.

SLYBOOTS = Crafty fellow.

PARTHIAN = Backward-looking [the Parthian horsemen of western Asia used to shoot their arrows backwards while in real or pretended flight from their enemies].

SNUFFY = Soiled with (or smelling of) snuff - finely powdered tobacco which was sniffed up the nose in small quantities as an alternative to smoking [Dutch Snuf, ´a sniffing´].

SPINDLE-SHANKED = Long-, thin-legged [Old English Spinel, ´thin rod´].

JASEY = Humorous name for a wig (especially one made of worsted, or long-staple wool used for stockings) [after the island of Jersey, which specialised in knitwear: 49°N, 2°W].

CHASSEUR = Attendant (or man-servant) dressed in military style [French, ´huntsman´].

CALASH = Hood (supported by hoops) projecting beyond the face;   a hat consisting of a cane or whalebone frame covered with silk, named after the hood of the French carriage called a caleche, but itself originally known as a Therese.

AGREMENS = Amusements.

BATTUES = Meetings to shoot at game-birds driven from cover by servants´ beating bushes.

FLAMBEAU = A flaming torch, made of thick wicks (or loose, spongy strings, which draw up the melted tallow or wax) covered in wax or tallow (hard animal-fat) [French, from <u>Flambe</u>, ´a blaze´; itself from Latin <u>Flamma</u>, ´a flame´].

CHAPTER 63

LEVÉE = Morning assembly (and ´morning´, till the twentieth century, denoted daylight events which in polite society took place after noon) at which the Sovereign received only men [French <u>Lever</u> (noun), ´Sovereign´s reception´; from Latin <u>Levāre</u>, ´to rise´ - the picture is of men rising from obeisance to their Sovereign].

CONTINGENT = Proportion of troops allotted to a commander [Latin <u>Contingens</u>, ´falling [to]´ - ´It fell to me to lead the first troop´, &c].

SIMPERING = Smiling in a silly, affected (´put-on´) way [Danish, <u>Simper</u>, ´coy´].

CAMBRIC = Fine white linen [originally made at Cambray (50.2^{o}N, 3.5^{o}E), forty miles south by east of Lille, in Flanders].

CORSAGE = Bodice [French]; the part of a dress to fit closely round the upper trunk.

WALKED A POLONAISE = Danced [Anglo-Saxon <u>Wealcan</u>, ´to turn about´].

QUARTERS = Known in heraldry as ´Seize quartiers´, the noblest families boast arms for two parents, four grandparents, eight great-grandparents and sixteen great-great-grandparents; all showing traces on one coat of arms.

JANISSARY = Turkish soldier [Turkish <u>Yeni</u>-, ´new´ + <u>Tcheri</u>, ´militia´: footguards originally composed of the sons of Christian slaves].

SOBIESKI = Jan Sobieski (1624-96) was elected King John III of Poland after defeating the Turks at Pilawiecz in 1674. His greatest victory was his relief of Vienna after a two-month siege in 1683.

AQUATIC INSURRECTIONS = Water-works, in the sense of intricate fountains [Latin <u>Aqua</u>, ´water´; <u>Insurrectionem</u>, ´uprising´ - here, in the sense of a structure].

CONCHES = Shells of a particular shape (imitated by cream-horns).

MOUNTEBANKS = Itinerant quacks (pedlars) who appeal to the crowd from a platform by telling them anecdotes, doing tricks and juggling, often with the help of a professional clown [Italian <u>Monta in banco</u>, ´Climb up on a bench´].

<u>LA PETITE VIVANDIERE</u> = One who follows an army to sell its soldiers food, drink and other provisions (for instance, needles and cotton).

WINDLASS = A revolving pole on which a rope was wound, for raising weights [Old Norse <u>Vindill</u>, ´a winder´; from <u>Vinda</u>, ´to wind´ + <u>Ass</u>, ´a pole´].

CONDITOREY = Repository (furniture store) [Latin <u>Conditōrium</u>, ´tomb´ - where the dead repose!].

OPHICLEIDES = A late eighteenth-century predecessor of the bassoon and tuba; in fact, a bass bugle with keys like a trumpet. Because it was an adaptation of the serpent (being a conical brass tube bent double), it was named from the Greek <u>Ophis</u>, ´snake´ + <u>Kleis</u>, ´key´. It was invented by M Frichot in London in c 1790.

HABITED = Dressed.

<u>AU FAIT</u> = After all; indeed.

THE ´SOMNAMBULA´ = The chef d´oeuvre of Vincenzo Bellini (1801-1835), written for the opera house of La Scala, Milan, and performed there in 1831. Thackeray thought of it because it was as popular in England as it was in Italy, and therefore his readers would know it; but, in <u>Vanity Fair</u>, it is an anachronism, for this is the summer of 1827.

PRODIGATED = Squandered; spent lavishly [Latin <u>Prōdigus</u>, ´wasteful´].

<u>DU</u> = You; but in a special sense which we have lost, found in the ´thou´ of Elizabethan times, and ´tu´ (as opposed to ´vous´) in French, indicating closeness of sympathy and habit.

CANONESS = A woman who receives revenue allotted for the performance of divine service in a Cathedral or collegiate church, without having to take religious vows [Latin <u>Canon</u>, ´rule´, in the sense of obedience to the laws of the Church].

<u>FÊTES</u> = Festivities; merry-makings; celebrations.

LAMPIONS = Pots of coloured glass containing oil with a wick, used in illuminations (lights after dark) [Italian <u>Lampione</u>, ´a big lamp,].

TRANSPARENCY = Picture on a translucent (light-passing) substance such as glass, with a light behind it.

<u>TRENTE-ET-QUARANTE</u> = Sometimes known as <u>Rouge-et-noir</u>: a card-game with a banker (or dealer), and four diamond-shaped spots on the table (two red, two black) on which bets are placed.

HANKERED = Hung; loitered [Dutch <u>Hunkeren</u>, ´to desire´].

CROUPIERS = Men who rake in the money at a gaming table [French <u>Croupe</u>, ´rump; hinder part´: the image, for quite subtly meaningful reasons which will occur to those who think of expressions like ´filthy lucre´ and ´made a pile´, is of one following horses with a bucket and spade].

PUNTERS = Those who play against the bank at faro and other games for money [Latin <u>Punctum</u>, ´a point´ on which bets are placed].

FLORINS = Ten-penny pieces in today´s currency; but always worth a tenth of a pound in English money, and brought into the currency with decimation in view. It had a different value in different countries [so-called because of the lily stamped on the first florins, the Italian word Flore meaning ´a flower´].

THRUMMING = Drumming her fingers on (a sign of nervous excitement).

MONSIEUR N´EST PAS JOUEUR? = ´M´sieur is not playing?´

EN MARQUIS = Dressed (quite improperly, we may be sure) as a marquis.

LAISSEZ—MOI TRANQUILLE. IL FAUT S´AMUSER, PARBLEU, &c = ´Leave me alone. One must amuse oneself, great heavens! I´m not M´sieur´s servant´.

NAPOLEONS = Gold coins worth twenty francs each.

COUP = Stroke (of luck).

CHAPTER 64

AHRIMANIANS = Worshippers of Ahriman (or Angra Mainyu); in the Zoro-astrian system of religious thought, the principle of evil, in perpetual conflict with Ormazd, god of goodness and light.

SIREN = The Sirens were creatures who looked like beautiful women, fabled to live on an island off the south-west coast of Italy, and lure sailors by their song to destruction on the rocks [Greek <u>Seirēn</u>].

TURBID = Muddy [Latin <u>Turbidus</u>, ´disturbed; stormy´].

SPAR = Mast; beam [Dutch].

MALEVOLENCE = Ill-will [Latin <u>Male</u>, ´ill´ + <u>Volens</u>, ´disposed´].

DOCTORS´ COMMONS = Divorce proceedings.

HOOPING-COUGH = Contagious disease whose symptoms include short coughs and long, noisy inward breaths - the hoop, now spelt whoop.

SLIP-SLOP = Tittle-tattle; trifling talk; gossip.

ALBION = The old, poetic name for England [Latin <u>Albus</u>, ´white [cliffs]´].

PACKET = Packet-boat, plying between two ports, to carry mail-bags (packets), goods and passengers.

NIGGARDLINESS = Meanness [Swedish <u>Njugg</u>, ´misery].

THE DARBYITE = Follower of The Revd John Nelson Darby (1800-82), educated at Westminster School and Trinity College, Dublin, who founded the Christian Brethren in (and here comes another anachronism, for the story has yet to reach year) 1830.

FEEJEE ISLANDERS = Now spelt Fiji. The islands will be found at the section of 18°S, 178°E.

COMMINATIONS = Warning of evil; denunciations [Latin <u>Commināri</u>, ´to menace´].

REPROBATE = Person condemned as worthless [Latin Re-, 'the opposite of' + Probātus, 'tested and approved'].

LARES = Household gods; things 'we swear by' and thoroughly trust. The work has two syllables: 'Lah-raise' [Latin Lār, 'tutelary deity'; Lares being the plural, 'deities'].

DAWS = Jackdaws: meaning, 'those who belonged' to these places.

THE EAGLES = Not the Eagleses [Mr & Mrs Eagles], but, in this sentence, Mrs Eagles.

PROTEGÉE = The person under her protection.

MÉNAGE = Household; groups living under the same roof.

DRAM = Dose; an eighth of an ounce (of opium, in this context). More often, as much liquor (in the form of spirits) as is drunk at once [Greek Drachmai, from Drassomai, 'to grasp with the hand'].

PLAQUES = Stars (as of a knightly order).

CORDONS = Ribbons or sashes (again, as of a knightly order).

ÉCARTÉ = Card-game for two, excluding cards to the values 2-6; so-called because players exchange their cards [French, 'discarded' - which means, to throw out of one's hand such cards as one intends not to play].

ENTRESOL = Low-ceilinged storey (whose rooms are occupied by servants) between two others of greater height (whose rooms are occupied by masters).

PORT-COCHÈRE = Gateway; main entrance.

ROUÉS = People devoted to pleasure to an extent which wins the disapproval of others; rakes; libertines [literally, 'people broken on the wheel' - an ancient instrument of torture, to which people were tied, which was revolved in such a way that they received a series of blows which broke their limbs. The idea is the thought, 'They were broken on the wheel; or, if they weren't, they ought to have been, because they were so wicked'; from French Rouer, 'to break on the wheel'].

FELICITOUS = Supremely happy and fortunate [Latin Fēlix, 'happy']. Thackeray is being sarcastic, for felicity is one of the very greatest ideas in human life: it is the sort of happiness which one might hope for in heaven; indeed, people talk of the state they have in mind as being 'in the seventh heaven'; and it ought to mean the highest and most perfect joy of which mankind is capable.

PENSIONS = Boarding-houses.

PENSION = Board and lodging; fee for food, drink and shelter.

SCORE = Bill [from the notch cut in a stick to keep tally of debts incurred, from Icelandic Skora, 'to number by notches'; more recently, chalk-marks after one's name on a slate].

KNAVERIES = Dishonesties [Anglo-Saxon Cnafa, 'a boy or youth'; one of several words which reveal that masculinity equals crime - or at least ugly manners. For example, churl means a man, in the special sense intended by women when they snort the word, 'Men!'].

<u>VIPERE</u> = Viper (which would bite you if you took it to your bosom; bosom meaning, not the breast, as people think, but the crook of one's arm [or, rather, the angle made by upper arm and shoulder, where one would lay the head of a child or an invalid whom one intended to nourish; see, for example, Luke 16:22-33].

ULYSSES = The hero of Homer's Iliad is known in Greek as Odysseus; his journeys were so extensive that any outstandingly long journey may be called an odyssey.

BAMPFYLDE MOORE CAREW = Son (1693-c 1759) of the rector of Bickleigh, near Tiverton, who ran away from school to join the gypsies, and eventually became their king.

BOHEMIAN = A gypsy (because the first gypsies to enter France were supposed to be Hussites - followers of the religious reformer, John Huss, who was burned to death in 1415 - driven from Bohemia, which became part of what was called Czechoslovakia in 1918); hence, any unconventional or disreputable person.

RAFFS = People of little worth; the scum of the community [French <u>Rif et raf</u>, 'one and all' - riff-raff].

ESTAMINETS = Coffee houses [French].

BRITZKAS = Large carriages which could be converted into sleeping compartments by raising the sides and hood: driven by postilions or from the box, with four or six horses [Polish <u>Bryczka</u>, diminutive of <u>Bryka</u>, 'goods wagon'].

MARTINGALE = System of doubling the stake [the money one is betting] when losing in gambling, to recoup [get back] one's losses.

MADAME DE CRUCHECASSÉE = 'Broken Vase'; slang for 'blockhead', or person who is [more slang] 'cracked'. Thackeray's names are intended to sum up an entire personality in a word, and only the more subtle need explaining.

HOCUSSED = Cheated [from <u>Hocus pocus</u>; a sham-Latin invocation by conjurors who are now more likely to say, 'Abracadabra'].

<u>MATINÉE MUSICALE</u> = Musical afternoon [more evidence that, in the nineteenth century, social events described as <u>Matin</u>, or morning, happened <u>apres midi</u>, or afternoon. There is a reason for this. It is only in the twentieth century that we have taken to correcting those who bade us, 'Good morning', should noon have passed, on the interesting supposition that a day has three parts: morning, afternoon and night. We are wrong: a day has two parts only: morning [all the hours of daylight, from Lithuanian <u>Mirgu</u>, 'to glimmer; to gleam'] and evening [whose root means, 'to retire to bed']; or forenoon [which lasts from midnight to noon] and afternoon [noon till midnight]. There is no logical justification for the notion of a three-part day, convenient as is the word afternoon to designate the interval between lunch and tea. The important thing to bear in mind is that there is a substantial part of the time after noon when it is still morning - that is, daylight.

<u>PARQUET</u> = Enclosure; the part of the ground-floor nearest the orchestra.

PUT TO SHIFTS = Hard put to it.

<u>TOPLITZ AND VIENNA</u> = Both in Austria: what is now Teplice at 50.6°N, 14°E, and Vienna at 48°N, 16°E.

BOX-OPENER = Attendant; what we should call an usherette, except that our age expects an adolescent where Thackeray's expected an anile attendant.

SCUDI = Silver coins worth four shillings [which would be 1, or even 2, today: from Portuguese Escudo, 'shield', itself from Latin Scutum; hence, 'embossed coin'].

WASH-BALLS = Balls of soap.

ESSENCES = Perfumes.

MONSIGNORI [pronounced ´ - seen-yaw-ri´] = Dignitaries.

BEARS = Rude men; unmannerly people.

BALDAQUINS = Canopies [Italian Baldacchino].

DILIGENCE = Stage coach [French].

FAUGH = One way of writing the sound which people have made down the ages on encountering a bad smell. Others are, 'Phew!', 'Phooey', and (in the psalms of The Book of Common Prayer) 'Fie upon thee'.

NYM AND PISTOL = See Henry V; especially the film of Shakespeare's play.

GIBBETED = Hanged [French Gibet, 'gallows'; diminutive of Gibe, 'a stick' - cf Jib].

ENTOMOLOGICAL COLLECTIONS = Collections of butterflies and moths [whose bodies are 'cut into' by a waist: Greek En-, 'into' + Tomos, 'cut' + Logia, 'discourse', in the sense of a body of learning, or 'things known about' something].

BON ENFANT = Good-natured.

PARÔLE D'HONNEUR = On my word [of honour].

BRAVOS = Hired assassins.

FOURGONS = Big coaches with much luggage-space and an enlarged box-seat, in which footmen, valets and maidservants (often with an armed escort) in the charge of a courier went ahead of their employers to unpack and get rooms ready ['baggage-wagon'].

LOUIS = Louis XIII gold piece, or louis d'or, equivalent to a Napoleon [twenty francs].

A KING CHARLES = A King Charles spaniel, which has curly hair ['spaniel' meaning 'Spanish dog'].

LIVID = Black and blue, as though bruised [Latin Lividus].

FACTOTUM = Short for the Latin phrase, 'Hominum facere tōtum', meaning 'Man of all work'.

SECRETAIRE = A piece of furniture in which private papers could be kept [secret], with a shelf for writing on, and drawers and pigeon-holes.

CHAPTER 65

SALLIED = Went; rushed [the word conveys the idea of vigour, from Latin Salīre, 'to leap; to spring forth', which became in French, Saillir, 'to issue forth suddenly'.

FÊTES = Festivities.

SMALL-BEER = Beer of a weak, poor or inferior quality, good enough for every day (which always has a poor ring to it: think of Coarse, which simply means what one is likely to meet in the 'course' of everyday life).

BROCADES = Fabric richly wrought with a raised pattern [Spanish Brocado, 'pricked'].

ÉTAT MAJOR = Manager.

BAGMAN = Commercial traveller, who carried samples in his bag.

TUMBLERS = Gymnasts [Middle English Tumbel; frequentative (form of verb indicating that the action happened often, as Whinny is the frequentative of Whine, and Dabble of Dab) of the Old English Tumbian, 'to fall': cf French Tomber].

COURIER = Travelling servant, whose duty was to make all the arrangements for his employer's journey.

SOURNOIS = Deceitful; underhand.

SCHLAFROCK = Night-shirt (what we now mean by a 'nightie') [German].

DOMINO = A hood worn in winter by priests; a loose cloak worn chiefly at masquerades [masked balls; receptions, with dancing, to which guests wore black masks round their eyes to lend glamour and mystery to the occasion], with a small mask covering the upper part of the face.

POMATUM = Scented ointment in which apples [French Pommes] were perhaps once an ingredient.

PIQUE = Wounded pride [French Piquer, 'to pierce or prick'].

MACHINATIONS = Plots; schemes [Latin Māchina, ´stratagem; trick´].

DEJEUNER A LA FOURCHETTE = Substantial breakfast.

AVERNUS = Lake of Campania, south-west Italy, filling the crater of an extinct volcano. The unpleasant vapours rising from its surface made the ancients suspect that it was the entrance to hell. It is hell that Thackeray has in mind here.

MINX = A pert [that is, originally, Apert = open (think of Aperture), with the idea of being too open, and therefore forward or cheeky), wanton (that is, unrestrained; uncontrolled; undisciplined) girl [possibly from the dialect Minikin, ´a little lass´]. The word shows the problem of being a girl to some extent; for girls are assumed by humanity to be acceptable and harmless in a way that boys are not; and that sometimes leads girls to seek attention by saying whatever comes into their heads. They get attention every time, and come to enjoy it so much that they would rather have a mixture of attention and disapproval than be forgiven and forgotten.

BLACKLEG = Swindler; card-sharper [one who cheats at cards].

LAUDANUM = Alcoholic tincture of opium [Paracelsus coined the name for a costly medicine in which opium was thought to be an active ingredient].

CHAPTER 66

ACCEPTANCE = Formal undertaking to pay a bill when it is due to be paid ['to take up' meant 'to extend the period of credit', or time when one need not pay].

RECRUITING = Restoring; renewing; giving strength and life (the place for such restoring is known in French as a restaurant).

BUTTERBRODS = Slices of bread and butter [German Butterbrot].

FUMUM = Smoke [Latin Fūmus].

STREPITUS = Noise; bustle [Latin].

PERNICIOUS = Very injurious [Latin Perniciōsus]. The expression 'pernicious vegetable' reminds us that smoking really was frowned on in Victorian society. Eden Philpotts captures the attitude in the sentence which he puts into the headmaster's mouth in one of the Human Boy stories: 'The inhalation of fumes resulting from the conflagration of a poisonous weed is a habit unworthy of a Christian and a gentleman'.

'FUCHS' = Fox [German].

'PHILISTER' = Philistine [meaning one who has no discernment of the arts].

EILWAGEN = Fast coach.

EN BAYS [PAYS] DE GONNOISANCE [CONNAISANCE] = Among friends; as we might say, 'He seems to be well in'.

IN NUBIBUS = In a multitude; among many (in other words, 'run of the mill'. Here we are, running down the world of every day again - as we do: 'Very ordinary').

BURSCHEN = Young fellows [German].

RENOWNER = 'One who celebrates'. Whoever is renowned is celebrated, in more senses than one; from Latin Re-, 'again' + Nōmināre, 'to name': as in, 'Here's to John'; and everyone raises his glass, and says, 'To John'.

SCHRECKLICH = Frightful [German].

SAUFEN = Tippling; boozing [German].

SINGEN = Singing.

MAWKISH = Sickly; likely to nauseate [from an old word meaning Maggotty].

DRAUGHT = Quantity of liquor swallowed in one go [early Middle English Draht, from Dragan, ´to draw or suck´].

CIRCE = Odysseus´s special enemy, who turned his men into pigs.

TOILS = Nets for catching birds; webs (as of spiders) [Latin Tēla, ´loom; weaving; what is woven´].

RETICULE = Hand-bag (originally of netting, as a workbag) [Latin Retīculum, diminutive of Rēte, ´net´].

SPOONEY = Foolish fellow [´needing to be spoon-fed´].

VIRAGO = Man-like woman [Latin].

CICATRIZED = Induced to form a scar [Latin Cicātrix, ´scar´].

IN FINE = In short [French Fin, ´(In the) end´]. The notion would be expressed in our phrase, ´when it comes to the crunch´.

GALIGNANI = Galignani´s Messenger; the English-language periodical published in Paris for sale to British tourists abroad.

QUERIST = Enquirer [Latin Quaerere, ´to seek; to inquire´].

REPAIRED = Went; betook himself [Latin Repatriāre, ´to return to one´s native land´].

PET = Temper; fit of ill-humour [possibly abbreviated from Petulans, ´attacking´].

CALUMNY = Malicious misrepresentation; slander; speaking evil of, falsely [Latin Calumnia, ´false accusation´].

MALIGNED = Spoke evil of [Latin Malus, ´evil´ + Genus, ´kind; type´].

SALLY = Attack [French Saillie, ´sudden leap or rush [as of troops from fortifications, to attack besiegers]´, from Latin Salīre, ´to leap´].

RANCOUR = Ill-will [Latin Rancor, ´bitter grudge; unpleasant odour [as of rancid food]´].

ABUTTING = Springing; jutting out [Old French Á, ´toward´ + Bouter, ´to thrust´].

REMARKED = Noticed; became aware of [French Re-, ´particularly´ (intensive prefix) + Marquer, ´to observe or regard´].

SYMPTOMS = Signs which are evidence of more than can be seen [Greek Sym- (Syn-), ´with´ + Piptein, ´to fall´, in the sense of things ´falling out together´, or happening simultaneously. If happenings always coincide, one can sometimes deduce what cannot be observed from whatever can].

RALLY = Tease; chaff [French Railler, 'to banter'].

PORTMANTEAUS = Travelling bags [French Porte-, 'carrying' + Manteaux, 'cloaks' or 'mantles'].

POSTILLION = Rider on the near leading horse of a carriage and four (or the near horse of a pair) [Italian Postiglione, 'post-boy']. There was fierce competition between the driving of postilions (drawing post-chaises and travelling chariots) and coachmen (who drove stage coaches from the box). The coachmen outlasted the postilions.

SCHIMMELS = Grey-white horses [German, 'mildew'].

CAMLET = Fabric [Arabic Khamlat, from Khaml, 'pile' or 'nap' - the tiny hairs arising from all cloth].

MANCHEN STURM ERLEBT = Weathered (= lived through) many a storm [German].

FORT = 'Drive on' [German].

SCHWAGER = 'Coachman' [German].

CHAPTER 67

PERTAINING TO = Concerning; having to do with [Latin <u>Pertinēre</u>, ´to belong´].

DROMEDARY = A swift kind of camel (the Arabian camel, which has one hump, as opposed to the Bactrian camel, which has two humps) [Greek <u>Dramein</u>, ´to run´]. Bactria was part of the old world now known as Wakhan, a district of Tadzhik north-east of Afghanistan; c 37°N, 73°E.

TENTS AND PILAU = In effect, food and shelter. Strictly, pilau is boiled meat, rice, raisins and spices [Persian <u>Pilaw</u>].

ISHMAELITE = One at war with society (see Genesis, chapter 16) - the ideal word here, because Ishmael was a rover through the desert, whose ´hand was against every man, and every man´s hand against him´.

´WERTHER´ = Novel by Johann Wolfgang von Goethe (1749-1832), whose full title is, <u>Leiden des jungen Werthers</u> (1774).

´WAHLVERWANDTSCHAFTEN´ = Strictly, <u>Die Wahlverwandtschaften</u> (1808). Both novels are fanciful to an extent which Thackeray mocks.

<u>DU</u> - ´Thou´ (the intimately friendly way of addressing people which English no longer possesses, but which French preserves in <u>Tu</u> as opposed to <u>Vous</u>).

MADE NO SCRUPLE OF = Thought nothing of; had no hesitation in [scruple comes from the Latin <u>Scrupulus</u>, ´a little pebble´: in other words, a very tiny thing to be anxious about].

<u>DISTRAITE</u> = Absent-minded.

PEEVISH = Fretful.

´EINSAM BIN ICH NICHT ALLEINE´ = ´Alone, I am not lonely´.

TRAINING OFF = Trailing.

BAND-BOXES = Boxes for bands (pieces of linen worn decoratively, as by an Anglican clergymen from his clerical collar), ribbons, and so forth, kept flat.

NANKEEN = Cotton cloth [originally woven at Nanking, southern capital of the province of Kiangsu in China: 32°N, 118°E].

TÊTE-A-TÊTE = Confidential talk; intimate discussion [French, 'head-to-head'].

FOND = Foolish; characteristic of a person infatuated [Old English Fonne, 'to be foolish'].

'GELIEBT UND GELEBET' = 'Lived and loved' (Johann Christoph Friedrich von Schiller, 1759-1805).

'WALLENSTEIN' = Said to be the greatest historical drama in the German language, the trilogy comprising Wallensteins Lager, Die Piccolomini and Wallensteins Tod ('Wallenstein's Camp', 'The Piccolomini' [literally, 'The little men'], and 'Wallenstein's Death') was written between 1796-99, and translated into English by Samuel Taylor Coleridge in 1800.

BOOMPJES = Waterfront [Dutch].

REDOUTES = Casinos [French].

GOURMANDIZE = Eat to excess; stuff themselves [French Gourmand, 'glutton'].

TABLES D'HÔTE = Literally, the host's tables. The distinction is between a set meal at a fixed time at a fixed price, and a la carte, where patrons selected each course from a list of possibilities at varying prices, and probably ate when they pleased. In Europe, what Thackeray called table d'hôte is signified by the phrase En pension - 'like a boarding-house'.

CHANCELLERIE = Legation; embassy [Latin Cancellārius, 'an usher who saw to it that no authorized person passed the bar of a court'].

MILCH COW = Cow kept for milking; person from whom money can easily be got.

CAME OFF WITH HER LARES = Took with her her most precious possessions [lares were originally household gods; from the Latin Lār, 'tutelary deity', of which Lares was the plural; pronounced Lah-raise.

BONES = Dice.

SPLIT = 'Give you away'; 'Tell on you'; 'Divulge your secret'.

BAMBOO-CANE = [The man who carries] the bamboo-cane (an example of synecdoche [si-nec-do-key]: referring to the whole of something by naming part of it; for example, 'All hands on deck'].

GABY = Simpleton; silly, foolish person [akin to Gape; Gab].

SHIVERED = Broken in pieces [German Schiefern, 'to splinter'].

'UN BIGLIETTO ECCOLO QUA!' = 'Look! Here is a note' (from Rossini's opera, The Barber of Seville, 1816).

UNDER WEIGH = Moving; on her way; therefore, under way [there is a common confusion with the expression, 'To weigh anchor', and so get on the move; but The Oxford Dictionary assures us that 'under weigh' is erroneous].

A DANDY TELESCOPE = A telescope so smart as to be <u>too</u> smart;   Oliver Goldsmith once wrote that to be seen to possess anything so expensive that one could not afford to get another like it was a sign of ill-manners: but perhaps Thackeray is just boyishly rejoicing on Georgy´s behalf that he had a telescope worth possessing.

A BLACK ECLIPSE = Possibly, simply a black shape.   J I M Stewart thinks ´eclipse´ a possible misprint for ´ellipse´.

Δαϰϱυόεν γελασάσα = Literally, ´she wept, having laughed´ (Homer);   probably, she wept for joy´, or, ´she laughed through her tears´, is Thackeray´s intention.

COMMISSIONER = Later called a commissionaire;   meaning a light porter, who attended to passengers and their luggage when steamboats docked.

BEAGLES = Small hunting-dogs used to hunt hares.

PUNJAUB = Part of what is now India proper [$30°N$, $75°E$].

CALUMNIES = Scandalous stories;   slanders [Latin, ´false accusation´].

MESSRS BURKE, THURTELL & HAYES = A rather sinister joke by Thackeray.   William Burke (1792-1829) - of Burke and Hare, who sold corpses to medical men who wanted to dissect them for purposes of study - John Thurtell (1794-1824) and Catherine Hayes (1690-1726) were all noted murderers;   so that Thackeray is implying that Rebecca is responsible for Joe´s death: in other words, somehow she killed him, as Thackeray forewarned us at the time of the charades in Chapter 51.

EXAMINATION = A legal inquiry with sworn testimony.